Sports Law in the Philippines

Sports Law in the Philippines

Ignatius Michael D. Ingles

This book was originally published as a monograph in the International Encyclopaedia of Laws/Sports Law.

Founding Editor: Roger Blanpain
General Editor: Frank Hendrickx
Volume Editor: Michele Colucci

Wolters Kluwer

Published by:
Kluwer Law International B.V.
PO Box 316
2400 AH Alphen aan den Rijn
The Netherlands
E-mail: lrs-sales@wolterskluwer.com
Website: www.wolterskluwer.com/en/solutions/kluwerlawinternational

Sold and distributed by:
Wolters Kluwer Legal & Regulatory U.S.
7201 McKinney Circle
Frederick, MD 21704
United States of America
E-mail: customer.service@wolterskluwer.com

ISBN 978-94-035-0776-7

e-Book: ISBN 978-94-035-0976-1
web-PDF: ISBN 978-94-035-0986-0

I write this for the Filipino athlete, my parents, my son, and my wife. May they continue to fight the good fight.

The Author

Ignatius Michael "Mickey" D. Ingles is a student-athlete-turned-lawyer.

He splits his time between working in the Law Firm of Ingles Laurel & Calderon, where he practices taxation, corporate, and sports law, and teaching as a full-time professor at the Ateneo de Manila University School of Law, the Philippines, where he teaches Constitutional Law, Taxation Law, Emerging Issues in Sports Law, and Robots, Artificial Intelligence, and the Law.

Mickey is the author of *Laws for Sports and the Sporty*, the definitive guide on Philippine sports law. He is the founder and editor-in-chief of *Batas Sportiva*, the first and only law blog dedicated to Philippine sports law, and sits as the only Filipino member of the *LawInSport* Editorial Board. He also writes for Spin.ph, the country's leading standalone sports website, and Rappler.com, a Philippine social news network.

Mickey also authored *Tax Made Less Taxing,* a best-selling textbook on Philippine taxation which is now in its third edition. He has also written various law journal articles on sports law, the law of religion, the law of robots, and the constitutional aspects of student social media use, which have been published in both the Philippines and the United States.

He graduated salutatorian from the Ateneo Law School, Makati, the Philippines, in 2012, where he was also given the St. Thomas More Award for the Most Distinguished Graduate. He ranked first in the 2012 Philippine Bar Exams. He obtained his LL.M. from the Georgetown University Law Center, Washington D.C., in 2016. He is a licensed attorney in the Philippines and the State of New York.

When not busy lawyering, Mickey can be found on the soccer field. He was the starting right-winger of the Ateneo Men's Football team that won a record three straight University Athletics Association of the Philippines (UAAP) championships during 2004–2006. He was the team captain during 2005–2006 and was named 2006 UAAP Athlete-Scholar of the Year.

He is also a published novelist. His young adult fantasy novel, *Alinam: Diego Domingo and the Mandato Ruiz*, was published in 2020 to roaring reviews.

He can be contacted via e-mail (imdingles@ilclaw.com.ph) or social media (@mickeyingleslaw on Twitter, Facebook, and Instagram).

Research Assistants

The Author

Jose Ryan S. Pelongco graduated from the Ateneo de Manila University, the Philippines, in 2010. He is currently a fourth-year law student at the Ateneo de Manila University School of Law. He is currently a part of the Board of Editors of the *Ateneo Law Journal*, a resident intern of the Ateneo Human Rights Center, and a cohead of Transportation for the Ateneo Central Bar Operations. He has published an article for the Ateneo Law Journal entitled *Republic v. Sereno: Revisiting Constitutional Qualifications for Impeachable Public Officers*, 63 Ateneo L. J. 70 (2018) coauthored with Atty. Ray Paolo D.J. Santiago.

Mary Anne A. Galang graduated from Silliman University with a degree in Bachelor of Science in Accountancy in 2014 and passed the CPA Board Exam in the same year. She is currently a fourth-year law student at the Ateneo de Manila University School of Law, the Philippines. She wrote and successfully defended her Juris Doctor thesis entitled *On the Basis of XY: Examining Biological Differences in Women as a Ground to Deny Participation in Sports Competitions*, which focused on the binary system of recognition of sex in Philippine sports and its implications on women's rights.

Alexa Monica P. Dabao is an associate at the Law Firm of Ingles Laurel & Calderon (ILC) and handles corporate, tax, and sports law cases. She passed the Philippine Bar in 2020 and obtained her Juris Doctor from the Ateneo Law School with an international law and development track. She was also an accomplished mooter for the Ateneo Society of International Law (ASIL), competing in the 2018 and 2019 Jessup Cups and the 2018 Asia Cup held in Tokyo, Japan. She also served as ASIL's Secretary-General in her graduating year. In 2015, she obtained her Bachelor of Science in Legal Management from the Ateneo de Manila University, where she also played for the Ateneo Women's UAAP Football Team. Currently, she judges various international moots such as Jessup, Stetson, FDI, and the ILC Cup.

Table of Contents

Table of Contents

List of Abbreviations

Philippine Jurisdictions

CTA	Court of Tax Appeals
RTC	Regional Trial Court

Sporting Organizations

BAP	Basketball Association of the Philippines
BCAP	Basketball Coaches Association of the Philippines
FIBA	Fédération Internationale de Basketball
FIFPro	Fédération Internationale des Associations de Footballeurs Professionnels
IFs	International Federations
IOC	International Olympic Committee
NBA	National Basketball Association
NCAA-P	National Collegiate Athletic Association
NPC PHIL	National Paralympic Committee of the Philippines
NSAs	National Sports Associations
PATAFA	Philippine Athletics and Track and Field Association
PBA	Philippine Basketball Association
PFL	Philippine Football League
PHI-NADO	Philippine National Anti-doping Organization
POC	Philippine Olympic Committee
PSC	Philippine Sports Commission
PSL	Philippine Superliga
PVL	Premier Volleyball League
SBP	Samahang Basketbol ng Pilipinas, Inc.
UAAP	University Athletics Association of the Philippines

Philippine Government Organizations and Officers

BI	Bureau of Immigration
BIR	Bureau of Internal Revenue
CHED	Commission on Higher Education
COP	Compliance Officer for Privacy

List of Abbreviations

DepEd	Department of Education
DOH	Department of Health
DOLE	Department of Labor and Employment
DPO	Data Protection Officer
DSWD	Department of Social Welfare and Development
DTI	Department of Trade and Industry
GAB	Games and Amusement Board
IATF	Inter-Agency Task Force on Emerging Infectious Diseases
IPO	Intellectual Property Office
LA	Labor Arbiter
LGU	Local Government Unit
NTC	National Telecommunications Commission
PIC	Personal Information Controllers
PIP	Personal Information Processors
SEADO	Single Entry Approach Desk Officer
SEC	Securities and Exchange Commission
Philippine Statutes	
DPA	Data Privacy Act of 2012
IPC	Intellectual Property Code
LGC	Local Government Code
NACBIA	National Athletes and Coaches Benefits and Incentives Act
NIRC	National Internal Revenue Code
RTLA	Retail Trade Liberalization Act of 2000
SAPA	Student-Athletes Protection Act
TRAIN	Tax Reform for Acceleration and Inclusion Act
Others	
ACR I-Card	Alien Certificate of Registration I-Card
AEP	Alien Employment Permit
AWDs	Athletes with Disabilities
CBA	Collective Bargaining Agreement
CBU	Collective Bargaining Unit
CEU	Centro Escolar University
CIR	Commissioner of Internal Revenue
FIBA ADR	Internal Regulations Governing Anti-doping
FLD-FAN	Formal Letter of Demand and Final Assessment Notices
G2K	G2K Corporation
HR	Human Resources
IAJ	In-A-Jiffy
ICT	Information and Communications Technologies

IRR	Implementing Rules and Regulations
LVPI	Larong Volleyball sa Pilipinas, Inc.
MCIT	Minimum Corporate Income Tax
NSDF	National Sports Development Fund
OPC	One Person Corporation
PAGCOR	Philippine Amusement and Gaming Corporation
PDRCI	Philippine Dispute Resolution Center, Inc.
POGO	Philippine Offshore Gaming Operations
PWP	Provisional Work Permit
RCC	Revised Corporation Code
RPC	Revised Penal Code
RPT	Real Property Tax
SEA Games	South East Asian Games
SEnA	Single Entry Approach
SWP	Special Work Permit
VAT	Value-Added Tax
VVSI	Viva Vintage Sports, Inc.
WADA	World Anti-Doping Agency

List of Abbreviations

Acknowledgments

I would first like to thank Ryan and Mary Anne for their hard work in cleaning this article up. Their attention to detail and ability to work under time pressure were admirable and are solid indicia of their future success as lawyers. I would also like to thank my mentee Alexa for her work in the updates. Alexa has been a great addition to our firm and has all the makings of a great lawyer.

This work could also not have been possible without the support of the Law Firm of Ingles Laurel and Calderon, the leading sports law firm in the Philippines, and the Ateneo Law School.

Finally, no amount of words can express my gratitude for the unceasing support of my parents and my wife.

Salamat

Acknowledgments

General Introduction

§1. General Background

1. When one mentions the Philippines to a non-Filipino, Philippine sports is not exactly the first thing that may come to mind. Beaches, yes. Mangoes, probably. But sports? Save for a few world-class athletes like the boxer Manny Pacquiao, the Philippines is not considered a sports powerhouse internationally. The country won its first Olympic gold medal in Tokyo 2020, when weightlifter, Hidilyn Diaz, carried the hopes of the entire nation on her broad shoulders and made us believe that golden promises could indeed be fulfilled.[1] The country does not fare as well as it would hope in regional competitions either; in nearly six decades of participating in the South East Asian Games (SEA Games), the Philippines has only come out on top twice—both times as the host country, in 2005 and most recently in 2019.[2] It has never qualified for the Fédération Internationale de Football Association World Cup. The highest it placed in the Fédération Internationale de Basketball (FIBA) World Cup was an impressive third place—but that was way back in 1954. To say that the Philippines is an underachiever in international sports is an understatement.

2. While its performance in international events might give the impression that the Philippines cares little about sports, nothing can be further from the truth. The Philippines is, in fact, no different from the more developed countries when it comes to its culture and its relationship with sports. A quick drive around any city or municipality in the country would show that basketball is *the* sport in the country. The country's love for the game is evident in Rafe Bartholomew's book, *Pacific Rims,*[3] where the American sportswriter talks about how the Philippines has embraced the game in practically every aspect of Philippine culture. The rivalries involved with basketball, and the fanfare that comes with them, mimic those in the United States and in Europe. The country's premier professional basketball league, the Philippine Basketball Association (PBA), was founded on the rivalry of Crispa and Toyota, the country's own version of the Celtics-Lakers Rivalry in the 1970s

---

1. Gretchen Ho, *A Purpose Bigger Than Gold*, Philippine Star (Jan. 1, 2022), https://philstarlife.com/self/631440-hidilyn-diaz-gold.
2. *See* Christian V. Esguerra, *Why Host Countries Dominate SEA Games, Falter in Next*, ABS-CBN News (Dec. 6, 2019), https://news.abs-cbn.com/sports/12/06/19/why-host-countries-dominate-sea-games-falter-in-next (which explains why host countries normally win the SEA Games).
3. *See* Rafe Bartholomew, *Pacific Rims: Beerman Ballin'in Flip-Flops and the Philippines' Unlikely Love Affair with Basketball* (2010).

and 1980s.[4] Not to be outdone, rivalries in amateur sports, particularly between the elite schools of Ateneo de Manila University and De La Salle University, have even reached the pages of international newspapers, such as *The New York Times*.[5]

3. Basketball aside, other sports have also caught on with Filipinos. Boxing is and has always been the top fighting sport in the country. Champion boxers, such as boxing legend, Gabriel "Flash" Elorde and the incomparable Manny Pacquiao, have spawned generations upon generations of young Filipinos training to be the next big thing in professional boxing, as amateur boxers look to emulate the silver medal performance of Mansueto "Onyok" Velasco in the 1996 Atlanta Olympic Games.[6] The storied tradition of Philippine boxing has crossed the gender gap as well, with Filipina boxer Nesthy Petecio winning silver in the featherweight division during the Tokyo 2020 Olympics.[7]

4. Philippine football has had its share of ups and downs. The performance of the Men's National Team has been outshadowed by the success of the Women's National Team, which has qualified for the 2023 World Cup in Australia and is currently the champions of South East Asia.[8] The men's football league, the Philippine Football League (PFL), currently has a roster of six to seven teams.[9]

5. The popularity of women's professional volleyball keeps on increasing by the year. The intense fandom over collegiate women's volleyball had ushered in two women's volleyball leagues—the Philippine Superliga (PSL) and the Premier Volleyball League (PVL).[10] Fans have flocked to these two leagues, following their college idols as they graduate into the professional scene. While the PSL and PVL considered themselves semiprofessional, they have all the qualities of a professional league, with their players earning hefty compensation for playing year-long volleyball.[11]

---

4. Norman Lee Riego, *Best of Five Series: The Rivalry That Gave Birth to the PBA*, ABS-CBN Sports (Apr. 12, 2015), http://sports.abs-cbn.com/basketball/news/2015/04/12/best-of-five-series-the-rivalry-gave-birth-pba-1744.
5. Rafe Bartholomew, *A Nation's Passion Lives in a Rivalry of Green v. Blue*, The New York Times (Sep. 23, 2007), http://www.nytimes.com/2007/09/23/sports/23rivalry.html.
6. Ronnie Nathanielsz, *Olympic Stories: Onyok Velasco*, Yahoo! News (Jul. 10, 2012), https://sg.news.yahoo.com/olympic-stories--onyok-velasco.html.
7. Mark Giongco, *Nesthy Petecio Takes Home Olympic Silver in Boxing*, Philippine Inquirer (Aug. 3, 2021), https://sports.inquirer.net/432030/nesthy-petecio-takes-home-olympic-silver-in-boxing.
8. Lorenzo del Carmen, *Filipinas Make History, Cop PH's First-ever AFF Women's Crown*, Tiebreaker Times (Jul. 17, 2022), https://tiebreakertimes.com.ph/tbt/filipinas-make-history-cop-first-ever-aff-womens-crown/245568.
9. *Welcome to PFL!*, Philippines Football League, https://www.pfltv.ph/info.
10. Mark Edward Lopez, *Defining the 2010s: Emergence of PVL, PSL and Spikers' Turf*, Fox Sports PH (Jan. 1, 2020), https://www.foxsports.ph/volleyball/1057564/defining-the-2010s-emergence-of-pvl-psl-and-spikers-turf/.
11. *Ibid.*

6. Collegiate sports are just as popular as professional or international sports in the Philippines. Some would say that collegiate sports are even more popular. Sponsors definitely agree. One needs only to tune in to a University Athletics Association of the Philippines (UAAP) basketball or volleyball game to see the influx of cash flowing into collegiate sports. The UAAP, an association of eight schools located in Metro Manila, leads the way in collegiate sports, with its basketball and volleyball games shown in nationwide media.[12] Ateneo de Manila University and De La Salle University, the rival two schools featured in *The New York Times*, are members of the UAAP.[13] The National Collegiate Athletic Association (NCAA-P), an association of ten schools in Metro Manila that prides itself as the oldest athletic association in the country, is slowly catching up with the UAAP, both in terms of coverage and fanbase.[14]

7. Other sports have also gained a following in recent years. eSports have dominated sports pages because of both its novelty and the winnings eSports players receive, with some players said to have amassed more than USD 500,000 in earnings playing video games.[15] The popularity of eSports has even made it a medal event in the 2019 SEA Games where the Philippines bagged three gold medals out of a possible six events.[16] While martial arts have always been a staple in Philippine sports, the recent successes of Eduard Folayang (mixed martial arts), Meggie Ochoa (jiu-jitsu), Agatha Wong (wushu), Pauline Lopez (taekwondo), and Junna Tsukii (karate) have once again cast the spotlight on different disciplines.[17] In the area of gymnastics, Carlos Yulo bounced back after a disappointing 2020 Tokyo Olympics with five golds in the 2022 Vietnam SEA Games, pushing gymnastics into the limelight and undoubtedly inspiring thousands of Filipinos to take to the mats and bar in the hope of being the next Yulo.[18]

8. Marathons and triathlons are also extremely popular in the Philippines. Not a month goes by without an endurance event or two being held in the wee morning hours for both weekend warriors and elite professionals to test their mettle in. First held in 1974 and still an annual event, the MILO® Marathon is by far the most

12. Kathleen de Villa, *Timeline: UAAP History*, Philippine Daily Inquirer (Aug. 31, 2019), https://business.inquirer.net/277964/timeline-uaap-history.
13. Bartholomew, *supra* note 5.
14. Julian Malonso, *NCAA History*, The Philippine Star, https://www.philstar.com/2011/06/01/698483/ncaa-history.
15. Vignesh Raghuram, *Top 10 Highest-Earning Filipino eSports Players of All Time*, AFK Gaming (Sep. 3, 2019), https://afkgaming.com/articles/esports/Blogs/2371-Top-10-highest-earning-Filipino-esports-players-of-all-time.
16. ABS-CBN Sports Staff, *2019 SEA Games eSports Closes with Record Numbers*, ABS-CBN Sports (Dec. 12, 2019), https://sports.abs-cbn.com/esports/news/2019/12/12/2019-sea-games-esports-closes-record-numbers-64330.
17. Michael Angelo S. Murillo, *Standout Moments (2)*, Business World (Jan. 1, 2019), https://www.bworldonline.com/standout-moments-2/.
18. Marc Anthony Reyes, *SEA Games: Carlos Yulo Gets Fifth Gold to Lead Ph Gymnastics to Best Finish in Recent Years*, Philippine Daily Inquirer (May 16, 2022), https://sports.inquirer.net/462741/sea-games-carlos-yulo-gets-fifth-gold-to-lead-ph-gymnastics-to-best-finish-in-recent-years.

popular marathon and has been the gold standard in Philippine marathons.[19] The popularity of these endurance events has made their winners instant celebrities. 2019 Ironman 70.3 Philippines-Cebu winner Nikko Huelgas and 2019 and 2022 SEA Games gold medalist Kim Mangrobang have their impressive achievements in the triathlon to thank for their growing number of fans and admirers.[20]

9. The history of the Philippines—having been a colony of Spain, a territory of the United States, occupied by Japan in World War II, and finding its own as a sovereign independent nation—is reflected in both its unique love of sports and its legal system.

§2. Sources of Sports Law

10. The guiding principle of Philippine sports law is none other than its Constitution. Article XIV devotes two sections to sports, to wit:

> SECTION 19. (1) The State shall promote physical education and encourage sports programs, league competitions, and amateur sports, including training for international competitions, to foster self-discipline, teamwork, and excellence for the development of a healthy and alert citizenry.
> (2) All educational institutions shall undertake regular sports activities throughout the country in cooperation with athletic clubs and other sectors.[21]

11. These constitutional provisions, beautifully written as they are, are unfortunately mere guidelines for legislation and not self-executory. They are merely aspirational ideals that require enacting laws to actually become hard sources of law. As such, one would have to look elsewhere for sources of sports law in the Philippines. As sports law in the Philippines is in its infancy and is not as developed as in other jurisdictions, the laws and legal precepts that guide Philippine sports can be found in three broad categories.

12. The first source is general laws and legal doctrines which are applied to sports-specific situations. Under this category fall the application of general legal subjects such as contract law, labor law, intellectual property, taxation, criminal law, and torts in the realm of sports. The sports law cases that have reached the Philippine Supreme Court, minimal as it is, have focused on the application of general laws in the context of sports.

13. The second source is legislation that pertains specifically to sports. Granted, while these laws are few, not widely known by the public, and not implemented as well as they should, these sports-specific laws do exist. Examples of these laws are

---

19. Nestlé MILO® Staff, *Greatest Milo Moments*, Nestlé, https://www.milo.com.ph/history.
20. *See* Joaquin Henson, *Huelgas Pins Olympic Hopes on Kims*, The Philippine Star (Jan. 13, 2020), https://www.philstar.com/sports/2020/01/13/1984379/huelgas-pins-olympic-hopes-kims.
21. Phil. Const. Art. XIV, §19(1) & (2).

the Student-Athletes Protection Act (SAPA)[22] and the National Athletes and Coaches Benefits and Incentives Act (NACBIA).[23]

14. The third source can be found in the rules and regulations of the various international federations, national sports associations (NSAs), and other sports associations and leagues. These have been a fertile venue for sports law issues to arise from, as these rules and regulations have a more direct impact and effect on athletes and other sports stakeholders. These issues usually involve eligibility, discipline, and sanctions. Unfortunately, the resolutions of issues arising from these rules and regulations are not readily available to the public, given they are not judicial decisions that are mandated for public consumption. At most, the public finds out through media reports, which have been helpful in educating the masses on the intricacies and importance of these rules and regulations. Two prime examples which primed the public both occurred in 2018, as FIBA sanctioned an up-and-coming basketball prodigy for doping[24] and a few months later penalized the Samahang Basketbol ng Pilipinas, Inc. (SBP) for a rather controversial brawl between the Philippine national basketball team and its Australian counterpart.[25] A recent example involved Olympic pole vaulter and Asian record holder EJ Obiena and his NSA, the Philippine Athletics and Track and Field Association (PATAFA), where a lengthy public battle over non-liquidation of funds finally ended in a settlement reached by mediation.[26]

15. These three sources and more specific examples are discussed at length throughout this study.

§3. SPECIFICITY OF SPORT

16. Philippine law rarely makes exceptions for sports. The general legal perception of sports is that it falls within the neutral application of laws. As sports law in the Philippines is not as developed as in other jurisdictions, any time legal issues arise in the field of sports, the first reaction is to apply existing legal doctrines, regardless of the proper "fit" of the application. Slowly, however, the public is becoming more and more aware that a bit of nuance is required when applying a non-sports-centric legal framework into the context of sports. Sometimes, a fair

22. *See* Student-Athletes Protection Act, Republic Act No. 10676 (2015).
23. *See* National Athletes and Coaches Benefits and Incentives Act, Republic Act No. 10699 (2015).
24. Camille B. Naredo, *Kiefer Ravena Suspended by FIBA over Banned Substance*, ABS-CBN News (May 28, 2018), https://news.abs-cbn.com/sports/05/28/18/kiefer-ravena-suspended-by-fiba-over-banned-substance.
25. Nick Atkin, *Fiba Decision on Philippines v. Australia Brawl: 13 Basketball Players Suspended after Fight at World Cup 2019 Qualifier*, South China Morning Post (Jul. 19, 2018), https://www.scmp.com/sport/other-sport/article/2155986/philippines-v-australia-basketball-brawl-fiba-suspends-13-players.
26. Lance Agcaoili, *EJ Obiena, Patafa, Reach Settlement after Successful Mediation-PSC*, Philippine Inquirer (Mar. 30, 2022), https://sports.inquirer.net/456608/ej-obiena-patafa-reach-settlement-after-successful-mediation-psc.

amount of malleability and imagination are required to find out how Philippine laws can deal with the emerging concept of the specificity of sport.

17. With that said, sports has contributed and carved out a number of exceptions to certain general laws. For example, national athletes and coaches are granted discounts on certain purchases, which are unavailable to the general public.[27] Another example is the tax exemption for prize money earned by athletes in international events sanctioned by their own NSAs.[28] These, however, are few and far between.

27. National Athletes and Coaches Benefits and Incentives Act, §4.
28. National Internal Revenue Code (as amended) (1997), §32(B)(7)(d).

Part I. Organization of Sport

Chapter 1. Sports Governance

§1. Governmental Institutions and Bodies

I. Philippine Sports Commission

18. Republic Act No. 6847 created the Philippine Sports Commission (PSC) in 1990, under the administration of then-President Corazon Aquino.[29] Attached to the Office of the President, the PSC is the primary policy setting and implementing agency of the Philippines. It has a threefold objective to:

(1) provide the leadership, formulate the policies and set the priorities and direction of all national amateur sports promotion and development, particularly giving emphasis on grassroots participation;
(2) encourage wide participation of all sectors, government and private, in amateur sports promotion and development; and
(3) supplement government appropriations for sports promotion and development.[30]

19. As the country's main policy setting and implementing agency for sports, the PSC, has numerous legally mandated functions, such as establishing relationships with interNSAs,[31] developing and maintaining sports facilities around the country,[32] establishing publicly funded sports complexes,[33] and coordinating with various local government units (LGUs) and officials to develop and initiate sports development programs in their respective jurisdictions.[34] The PSC is also mandated to spearhead the search to honor exceptional Filipino athletes by setting up a screening committee that chooses members of the Philippine Sports Hall of Fame.[35]

29. *See* The Philippine Sports Commission Act, Republic Act No. 6847 (1990).
30. *Ibid.*, §6.
31. *Ibid.*, §7(b).
32. *Ibid.*, §7(d).
33. *Ibid.*, §7(e).
34. *Ibid.*, §7(m).
35. An Act Establishing the Philippine Sports Hall of Fame and Appropriating Funds Therefore, Republic Act No. 8757, §4 (1999).

20. While its main function is to impose policies to enhance sports participation and performance, the PSC also functions as the main governmental funding source of Philippine sports. The PSC's funds are mainly sourced from the Annual General Appropriations Act passed by Congress every year. The annual budget from Congress in 2022 was around PDP 825 million.[36] To augment the budget allocated by Congress, the PSC also receives a legally mandated portion of the gross income of the Philippine Amusement and Gaming Corporation (PAGCOR),[37] a government-owned and controlled corporation in charge of regulating gambling and casinos in the Philippines. PSC's funds are collectively called the National Sports Development Fund (NSDF), and as its name suggests, the NSDF serves as the coffer that finances the sports events in which the Philippines participates. This includes hosting the SEA Games and sending delegates to the Asian Games and the Olympics.[38]

21. The PSC has discretion on how it wishes to use or allocate the NSDF. For example, the PSC approved and allocated PDP 600 million of its budget for NSAs in 2018. Out of this PDP 600 million, PDP 220 million was earmarked and given to the NSAs of top-tier sports, which the PSC determined to be the country's best bets in garnering international acclaim and medals.[39] These sports include weightlifting, judo, taekwondo, gymnastics, and swimming.[40] PDP 140 million was allocated to the NSAs of second-tier sports, like jiu-jitsu, pencak silat, bowling, and golf.[41] The remaining PDP 240 million was shared by third-tier sports, such as football, dance sports, cycling, tennis, wrestling, volleyball, basketball, and handball.[42] Interestingly, the country's gold medalists in the 2018 Jakarta Palembang Asian Games hailed from a top-tier sport (Hidilyn Diaz for weightlifting), a second-tier sport (Lois Kaye Go, Bianca Pagdanganan, Yuka Saso for team golf, and Yuka Saso again for individual golf), and a sport that was notably absent in any of PSC's press releases on its budget (Margielyn Didal for skateboarding).[43]

22. The PSC also enjoys numerous tax benefits and incentives. It is exempt from the customs and tariff duties for the importation of international-standard sports equipment which are not otherwise locally available and are for the use of sports development and national athletes.[44] The same exemption is also available to NSAs,

36. Beatrice Go, *Ph Team Budget Increased for Jam-Packed 2022 Campaign*, Rappler.com (Sep. 30, 2021), https://www.rappler.com/sports/house-senate-increase-philippine-sports-commission-2022-budget/.
37. The Philippine Sports Commission Act, §26.
38. *Ibid.*
39. Reuben Terrado, *PSC Approves P600 Million Budget for NSAs with P220M Going to "Top-Tier Sports,"* Spin.ph (Mar. 29, 2018), https://www.spin.ph/multisport/psc-600-million-budget-nsas-2018-top-tier-sports.
40. *Ibid.*
41. *Ibid.*
42. *Ibid.*
43. ABS-CBN News Staff, *LIST: The All-Time Filipino Gold Medalists in the Asian Games*, ABS-CBN News (Sep. 2, 2018), https://news.abs-cbn.com/sports/09/02/18/list-the-all-time-filipino-gold-medalists-in-the-asian-games.
44. The Philippine Sports Commission Act, §19.

as long as these are certified by the PSC.[45] To encourage private funding, the law also exempted all donations to the PSC and certified NSAs from donor's tax.[46] These donations can also be deducted in full from the donor's income tax liabilities at the end of the taxable year.[47]

23. In terms of dispute settlement, the PSC is empowered "to exercise supervisory and visitorial powers over national sports associations."[48] However, it is important to note that these supervisory and visitorial powers are limited to only two instances: those "in connection with their sports promotion and development programs … "[49] and "with respect to which financial assistance is extended by the [PSC]."[50] The Implementing Rules and Regulations (IRR) of the PSC further expound on this power.[51] The PSC may resolve complaints filed against NSAs before the PSC on "mishandling of financial assistance … ,"[52] "intra-corporate conflict … ,"[53] and "physical and mental sexual abuse of athletes … ."[54]

24. The PSC is also empowered to "impose sanctions upon any national sports association, institution, association, body, entity, team, athlete and sports official for violation of its policies, rules and regulations … ."[55] These sanctions are in the form of suspending financial assistance to NSAs with ongoing intra-corporate disputes[56] and suspending allowances to non-performing athletes. The PSC mediated and helped settle the public spat between Olympic pole vaulter EJ Obiena and PATAFA in early 2022.[57]

25. The PSC is led by its Chairman and four Commissioners, all of which are appointed by and serve under the pleasure of the President.[58] The Chairman and Commissioners must be at least 30 years old, possess good moral character, and be publicly recognized in the field of sports.[59] The current Chairman is William I. Ramirez, who was appointed by President Rodrigo Duterte soon after assuming the presidency in 2016. Ramirez succeeds Ricardo R. Garcia, who served during 2010–2016 under the administration of President Benigno Aquino III.

45. *Ibid.*
46. *Ibid.*, §20.
47. *Ibid.*
48. *Ibid.*, §11(j).
49. *Ibid.*
50. *Ibid.*
51. Implementing Rules and Regulations of Republic Act No. 6487, Otherwise Known as the "Philippine Sports Commission Act" (2008) (hereinafter "PSC IRR").
52. *Ibid.*, Rule IV, §3(h).
53. *Ibid.*
54. *Ibid.*
55. *Ibid.*, §2(m).
56. *Ibid.*, §3(a).
57. Lance Agcaoili, *EJ Obiena, Patafa, Reach Settlement after Successful Mediation-PSC*, Philippine Inquirer (Mar. 30, 2022), https://sports.inquirer.net/456608/ej-obiena-patafa-reach-settlement-after-successful-mediation-psc.
58. The Philippine Sports Commission Act, §8.
59. *Ibid.*, §9.

26. The PSC is also responsible for planning and overseeing a program "to enable the Philippines to bid for a host the Olympic Games at the earliest practicable time."[60] As of this writing, this "earliest practicable time" has yet to come, as the Philippines has not yet placed any bids to host any Olympic Games.

II. Philippine Olympic Committee

27. While the main thrust of the PSC is the national development of sports, the Philippine Olympic Committee (POC) has a more limited, albeit important, purpose. True to its name, the main aim of the POC is to "develop and protect the Olympic Movement in the Philippines in accordance with the Olympic Charter."[61] It also aims to fight doping in sports[62] and to erase any form of discrimination and violence in sports.[63]

28. The POC is in charge of the country's involvement and participation in the Olympic Games.[64] It is recognized by the International Olympic Committee (IOC) as being the sole representative of the Philippines in international sporting events like the Olympics, the Asian Games, and the SEA Games.[65] Unlike the PSC, the POC is private in character and autonomous from the government.[66] This autonomy is recognized in the enacting law of the PSC.[67]

29. The POC is composed of members of the IOC in the country, distinguished Filipinos who enable the POC to perform its tasks, athletes who take part in the Olympics, and NSAs, whether included in the Olympic program or not.[68] The POC may also recognize other sports associations, which are not necessarily NSAs.[69] These members make up the POC General Assembly.[70]

30. Membership in the POC is coveted, given that only recognized NSAs can field national athletes in international events. Membership is by no means automatic. In determining membership with the POC, two rules must be remembered:

60. *Ibid.*, §7(c).
61. Philippine Olympic Committee Constitution and By-Laws, Art. I, §1(a) (hereinafter "POC Constitution").
62. *Ibid.*, §1(i).
63. *Ibid.*, §1(h).
64. Philippine Olympic Committee Staff, *About the POC*, Philippine Olympic Committee, https://www.olympic.ph/about-the-poc.
65. *Ibid.*
66. *Ibid.*
67. The Philippine Sports Commission Act, §12.
68. POC Constitution, Art. 4, §1.
69. *Ibid.*, §1(b.2).
70. *Ibid.*, Art. 6, §1.

first, the POC will only recognize one NSA for each sport under an IF,[71] and second, membership will only be granted after application by the NSA and approval by at least a two-thirds vote of the POC General Assembly.[72]

31. As the POC is "the final arbitrator of all intra-NSA conflicts and disputes … ,"[73] it has seen its fair share of membership controversies to resolve. In late 2018, it lifted the suspension of Philippine Swimming, Inc., the country's swimming NSA, after the NSA finally resolved its internal leadership issues under the supervision of the POC.[74] The POC has also recently resolved issues regarding the recognition of Larong Volleyball Sa Pilipinas Inc. (LVPI) as the NSA for volleyball and leadership of the Philippine Bowling Federation.[75] In 2020, the POC recognized the Philippine Electronic Sports Organization (PESO) as the NSA for eSports in the Philippines.[76]

32. Membership is also key in determining who will fall under the jurisdiction of the POC Ethics Commission. It was created in line with the POC Code of Ethics[77] and was formed to ensure that the POC and its member NSAs uphold the dignity, integrity, and ideals of the Olympic movement.[78] It is composed of five members—two of which are POC members.[79] It has the power to investigate and hear complaints[80] and mete out sanctions like warnings and reprimands.[81] However, the powers of the POC Ethics Commission are limited only to member NSAs.

---

71. *Ibid.*, Art. 4, §2.
72. *Ibid.*, §5.
73. *Ibid.*, Art. 3, §1(m).
74. June Navarro, *PSI Preparations Go Full Blast for 2019 PH SEA Games*, Philippine Daily Inquirer (Nov. 27, 2018), https://sports.inquirer.net/329119/psi-preparations-go-full-blast-for-2019-ph-sea-games?utm_expid=.XqNwTug2W6nwDVUSgFJXed.1.
75. Joaquin M. Henson, *Resolving NSA Disputes*, The Philippine Star (Oct. 9, 2018), https://www.philstar.com/sports/2018/10/09/1858563/resolving-nsa-disputes.
76. *PESO Named Official National Sports Association for eSports in the Philippines*, Spin.ph (Oct. 16, 2020), https://www.spin.ph/esports/peso-named-official-nsa-for-esports-in-the-philippines-a1373-20201016.
77. Philippine Olympic Committee, *POC Code of Ethics*, Tech Cellar, http://www.techcellar.com/olympic/wp-content/uploads/2015/10/codeofethics.pdf?__cf_chl_jschl_tk__=220e64ca9a73409b2cad93af73e194f75a2576e7-1579500784-0-AY6y4OLyZFiIKYZw0qxzxkjIFfrUeBqV3OGaX0si7Gl2kVNQkPGA74T0feQih8B1y7eAvbeurof7cBCBHFL-UxRabwn5bTWedW106M8lGA2vcD8OvjoEt3VGS8uCrB_XzM6eYahDMzuiYvk7-9hiJzUnTvT8e_0Iqo9tyKsaSHzyOGPuSQXe3mIMGViZA7JdNYcYqjWk2bCW9KDkqbf1hWAyDUpKFXmnZ2Sr0cHGVaZ4tRusDY40CqifaYFmXxLcOehlG4jDsYpeBoiXLnrTCA_9mW8XD_D-j4TZ4iHniuL96aN3RdqKh8GeXyXK6bUoq_M93-QK3RZ1gxPqJ5cXbTM.
78. Philippine Olympic Committee Ethics Commission, *Statutes of the POC Ethics Commission*, Philippine Olympic Committee, https://web.archive.org/web/20130108210349/http://www.olympic.ph/statutes.pdf.
79. *Ibid.*
80. Philippine Olympic Committee Ethics Commission, *Rules of Procedure Governing the Investigation of Cases Brought Before the POC Ethics Commission*, Philippine Olympic Committee, https://web.archive.org/web/20130129212257/http://www.olympic.ph/procedure.pdf.
81. *Ibid.*

33. The leadership of the POC has also been contentious. In 2016, longtime President, Jose Cojuangco, Jr., won the elections for an unprecedented fourth term. However, the Regional Trial Court (RTC) of Pasig invalidated his election due to some irregularities and ordered a new election to be held in February 2018. When the court-mandated elections were finally conducted, Ricky Vargas, the head of the Association of Boxing Alliances in the Philippines, emerged victorious with a 24-15 vote in his favor.[82] Vargas served as President of the POC until he resigned in 2019. The current POC President is Abraham "Bambol" Tolentino, a politician who won his bid for city mayor of Tagaytay City, Batangas, in the 2022 National Elections.

III. Games and Amusements Board

34. The Games and Amusement Board (GAB) is the government agency tasked with regulating and supervising professional sports in the country.[83] It was created in part to promote professionalism, prevent illegal game practices (like illegal betting and match-fixing), and supervise the operation and conduct of professional sports and their participants.[84] Aside from regulating professional sports, the GAB also supervises horse races and betting operations over these[85] cockfighting[86] and anti-illegal gambling operations in sports.[87]

35. Its regulatory functions extend to sports it has recognized as professional. The GAB-recognized professional sports include basketball, cycling, golf, billiards, dance sport, table tennis, mixed martial arts, Muay Thai, boxing, and motocross racing, to name a few. It has also recently recognized eSports as a professional sport under its regulatory powers.

36. As part of its regulatory functions, the GAB requires organizers of professional sports to apply and secure a permit, along with the payment of the necessary fees. Under Presidential Decree No. 871, it is illegal for any person, entity, or association to conduct professional games without a permit issued by the GAB.[88] Professional athletes must also secure a GAB license before engaging in professional sports. In fact, a GAB license is a condition for employment not only for players but also for referees, scorers, timekeepers, or other persons performing duties connected to professional games.[89] The persons required to obtain a license will require

82. Dennis Gasgonia, *Ricky Vargas Elected New PH Olympic Committee President*, ABS-CBN News (Feb. 23, 2018), https://news.abs-cbn.com/sports/02/23/18/ricky-vargas-elected-new-ph-olympic-committee-president.
83. Games and Amusements Board Staff, *Historical Background*, Games and Amusements Board, https://gab.gov.ph/historical-background/.
84. *See Philippine Basketball Association v. Gaite*, 608 Phil. 670 (2009).
85. *See* Creating the Philippine Racing Commission, Presidential Decree No. 420 (1974).
86. *See* Streamlining of the Office of the President, Executive Order No. 149 (1993).
87. *See* Strengthening the Operations of the Anti-Illegal Gambling Unit of the Games and Amusements Board, Administrative Order No. 222 (1995).
88. Placing Professional Basketball Games and Other Professional Games under the Supervision and Regulation of the Games and Amusements Board, Presidential Decree No. 871, §3 (1976).
89. *Ibid.*, §4.

per sport, as the GAB recognizes that different sports will each have their own sport-specific positions. The amount of the license fees to be paid will also depend on the sport and the position.

37. The GAB lists the requirements needed to secure a license. Again, this will depend on the sport. Notable among these requirements is passing a drug test. The drugs tested for are marijuana and methamphetamine, both considered illegal under Philippine laws.[90] This drug test requirement stirred a bit of controversy in early 2018 when Valve Corporation rescinded the Major designation of Defense of the Ancients 2 tournament that was slated to be held in Bulacan. The eSports developer cited the drug test as an infringement of players' privacy rights, especially for professional eSports athletes arriving in the Philippines to compete.[91] Some considered this a big deterrence to attracting world-class athletes and major professional events in the Philippines, while some stated that the GAB requirements were needed to legitimize eSports.[92]

38. Interestingly, the Valve pullout was not the first time a major sporting event was marred in a drug test-related controversy. In 2016, the Ultimate Fighting Championship canceled a fight card that was set to highlight a match between BJ Penn and Ricardo Lamas. Rumors flew around shortly thereafter, stating that the reason behind the cancelation was the government-imposed drug test. The UFC denied the allegation, stating that BJ Penn's injury forced them to postpone the fight. The GAB vehemently denied it as well, claiming the drug test requirement had been in place for years and that the rumors were spread to discredit President Rodrigo Duterte's war on drugs.[93]

39. The length of validity of the professional license for athletes like basketball players, boxers, and mixed martial artists is a year. Licenses must be renewed annually before the last day of March.[94] A penalty of 50% of the basic license fee is imposed on late renewals, and athletes must have a valid and existing license before participating in any promotion.[95] However, the GAB may revoke the license at any

---

90. Games and Amusements Board Facebook Page, *Clarification from the Games and Amusement Board*, Games and Amusements Board (Jan. 5, 2018), https://www.facebook.com/GamesandAmusementsBoard/photos/pcb.1517528191677934/1517527298344690/?type=3&theater.
91. Victor Barreiro Jr., *Valve Rescinds PH "Dota 2" Tournament's Major Designation*, Rappler (Jan. 5, 2018), https://www.rappler.com/technology/news/192948-valve-revokes-ph-dota-2-tournament-major-designation.
92. *Ibid.*
93. Nissi Icasiano, *UFC Rep Denies Drug Testing Led to Manila Event's Cancellation*, Rappler (Oct. 8. 2016), https://www.rappler.com/sports/by-sport/other-sports/148498-ufc-drug-testing-manila.
94. Games and Amusement Board Webpage, *Professional Basketball and other Professional Sports Division FAQs,* https://gab.gov.ph/professional-basketball-and-other-professional-sports-division-faqs/.
95. *Ibid.*

time. If the GAB has reason to believe that the holder has been guilty of dishonest practices, or has violated any laws, or for any just cause, they can revoke one's professional license.[96]

40. Professional sports leagues must also have their respective rules and regulations approved by the GAB. The GAB has the power to approve or disapprove rules and regulations on the operation and conduct of professional games.[97] An additional requirement is the remittance of 3% of gate receipts to the GAB. Any person, entity, or association conducting professional basketball games or other professional games must remit 3% of the gross gate receipts to the GAB to defray its expenses.[98] Aside from its share from gate receipts, the GAB is also entitled to 3% of income from TV, radio, and movie rights of professional games.[99]

41. This 3% remittance was the crux of the controversy in *Philippine Basketball Association v. Honorable Manuel Gaite,* a case decided by the Supreme Court in 2009.[100] In this case, the PBA entered into a Memorandum of Agreement with Viva Vintage Sports, Inc. (VVSI) for the exclusive rights to broadcast PBA games on television and radio for the 2000–2002 PBA seasons. In exchange for the rights, VVSI promised to pay PBA franchise fees. However, after a year, VVSI began to default in its payments repeatedly. In turn, PBA failed to pay the 3% share of the GAB, arguing that their remittance was conditioned on the actual receipt of franchise fees from VVSI. As VVSI failed to pay, argued PBA, then it was under no obligation to pay the GAB. Upon adjudication in the Office of the President, then Deputy of Legal Affairs Manuel Gaite ruled that the remittance to the GAB was *not* conditioned on actual receipt of franchise fees and that the GAB's right to collect their 3% share was not dependent on the PBA's ability to collect franchise fees from its franchisees, such as VVSI. The PBA sought to have Gaite's decision overturned but lost in the Supreme Court due to a procedural error.

42. As professional boxing is popular in the Philippines, thanks to the success of boxers like Gabriel "Flash" Elorde, Manny Pacquiao and Nonito Donaire, the GAB has a division devoted to boxing and other contact sports. The GAB oversees the ratings of Filipino boxers and has even entered into a Memorandum of Agreement with the Department of Health (DOH) to provide free medical and diagnostic examinations for professional boxers.[101] The efforts of the GAB toward Philippine boxing were recently recognized internationally, as the World Boxing Council named it the Commission of the Year for 2017.[102]

---

96. Presidential Decree No. 871, §4.
97. *Ibid.*, §2(c).
98. *Ibid.*, §8.
99. *Ibid.*
100. *Philippine Basketball Association*, 608 Phil. 670.
101. Department of Health Staff, *DOH & GAB Ink Agreement to Support Pinoy Boxers and Mixed Martial Artists*, Department of Health, https://portal2.doh.gov.ph/node/14969.
102. Carlos Costa, *Games and Amusements Board Is 2017 World Boxing Council's Commission of the Year*, Games and Amusements Board, http://gab.gov.ph/wbcs-commission-of-the-year-for-2017/.

43. The GAB is attached directly to the Office of the President. As such, orders, rulings, and decisions of the GAB must be appealed to the Office of the President within seventy-two hours, or else the order, ruling, or decision will be deemed final and unappealable.[103] The GAB Chairman is a presidential appointee. The outgoing GAB Chairman is Abraham Kahlil B. Mitra, who was appointed by President Duterte.

IV. National Sports Associations

44. NSAs are private organizations mandated to take charge of the development of their respective sports.[104] These NSAs are independent entities which have their own Constitutions and Bylaws. As part of their vital role as the main governing and regulating bodies of their respective sports, they organize competitions, recruit athletes for international competitions, and provide assistance to various sectors for the development of their sports, among others.[105]

45. While there may be multiple organizations which wish to develop their respective sports, there can be just one recognized NSA per sport. As mentioned previously, the POC recognizes a certain organization as the NSA of a sport by granting it membership. NSAs generally also have to be recognized by the IF of their particular sport. This requirement often leads to confusion about which organization is truly recognized by the IF and consequently should be recognized by the POC in order to be considered a regular member in its ranks.[106] For example, a controversy had continued between two competing volleyball organizations (LVPI and the Philippine Volleyball Federation) for recognition by the Fédération Internationale de Volleyball for years. The controversy has seemingly been put to rest with the recent POC recognition of the Philippine National Volleyball Federation, an NSA which promises to bring unity to various volleyball factions in the country.

46. The recognition of an organization as *the* NSA of a particular sport brings certain exclusive benefits. First, only organizations recognized as NSAs can field national athletes in international events like the Olympics. Second, NSAs may receive government funding from the PSC when the latter deems it necessary.

47. Table 1 provides a list of current NSAs divided by category.

103. Presidential Decree No. 871, §10.
104. Philippine Olympic Committee Staff, *Our NSAs*, Philippine Olympic Committee, https://www.olympic.ph/national-sports-association-regular-members/.
105. *Ibid.*
106. POC Constitution, Art. IV, §1.

Table 1 List of Current NSAs recognized by the POC

Regular Members	*Associate Members*	*Recognized Members*
World Archery Philippines, Inc.	Dance Sport Council of the Philippines	Philippine Windsurfing Association, Inc.
Philippine Amateur Track and Field Association, Inc.	Philippine Duckpin Bowling Center	National Motorcycle Sports and Safety Association
Philippine Badminton Association—Smash Pilipinas	Jiu-Jitsu Federation of the Philippines	Philippine Finswimming Federation, Inc.
Philippine Amateur Baseball Association	Powerlifting Association of the Philippines	Wakeboarding & Waterski Association
Samahang Basketball ng Pilipinas	Philippine Tournament Bridge Philippines	American Tackle Football Association of the Philippines, Inc.
Billiard & Sports Confederation of the Philippines	Philippine Cricket Association	Philippine Obstacle Sports Federation
Philippine Bowling Federation	Pilipinas Sambo Federation, Inc.	World Sikaran Brotherhood of the Philippines
Association of Boxing Alliances in the Philippines, Inc.	United Philippine Surfing Association	Philippine Floorball Association
Philippine Canoe-kayak Federation	Skateboarding and Roller Sports Association of the Philippines, Inc.	Philippine Kiteboarding Association
National Chess Federation of the Philippines	3D Air Sports and Hobbies Association, Inc.	Tchoukball Association of the Philippines
Integrated Cycling Federation of the Philippines	Samahang Kickboxing ng Pilipinas, Inc.	Automobile Association of the Philippines
Equestrian Association of the Philippines	Philippine Eskrima Kali Arnis Federation, Inc.	
Philippine Fencing Association, Inc.		
Philippine Football Federation		

Regular Members	*Associate Members*	*Recognized Members*
National Golf Association of the Philippines		
Gymnastics Association of the Philippines		
Philippine Handball Federation		
Pilipinas Larong Hockey, Inc.		
Philippine Judo Federation		
Philippine Lawn Bowls Association		
Muaythai Association of the Philippines, Inc.		
Philsilat Sports Association, Inc.		
Philippine Rowing Association		
Philippine Rugby Football Union, Inc.		
Philippine Sailing Association		
Philippine Skating Union		
Pilipinas Sepaktakraw Association, Inc.		
Philippine National Shooting Association		
Philippine Soft Tennis Association		
Amateur Softball Association of the Philippines		
Philippine Squash Academy, Inc.		
Philippine Swimming, Inc.		

Regular Members	*Associate Members*	*Recognized Members*
Philippine Table Tennis Federation, Inc.		
Philippine Taekwondo Association		
Philippine Tennis Association		
Triathlon Association of the Philippines		
Philippine National Volleyball Federation, Inc.		
Samahang Weightlifting ng Pilipinas		
Wrestling Association of the Philippines		
Wushu Federation of the Philippines		
Philippine Netball Federation, Inc.		

Sources: Philippine Olympic Committee Staff, *Regular Members*, Philippine Olympic Committee, https://www.olympic.ph/national-sports-association-regular-members/; Philippine Olympic Committee Staff, *Associate Members*, Philippine Olympic Committee, https://www.olympic.ph/national-sports-association-associate-members/; & Philippine Olympic Committee Staff, *Recognized Members*, Philippine Olympic Committee, https://www.olympic.ph/national-sports-association-recognized-members/.

48. Similar to leadership controversies in the POC, leadership issues also plague some NSAs, given the influence and prestige of certain NSAs. In 2009, leadership over the NSA of basketball even reached the Philippine Supreme Court.

49. In *Villafuerte v. Moreno*, the two feuding rival basketball associations in the Philippines, the Basketball Association of the Philippines (BAP) and *Pilipinas Basketbol* entered into a Joint Communique along the sidelines of the eighteenth FIBA World Congress held in Tokyo, Japan. The main objectives of the Communique were to unify the rival groups—essentially providing for their merger—and expedite the lifting of the FIBA-imposed suspension preventing the Philippines from participating in any international basketball competitions

50. Thus, the SBP was born. However, dissensions marred the creation of the supposed unified body, as its transitory President, Manuel V. Pangilinan, did not recognize the election of Luis R. Villafuerte as transitory Chair on account of the alleged failure of the latter to qualify for the said position. Eventually, Villafuerte and his group reported this alleged refusal to recognize him as Chair of the FIBA. At the same time, the Villafuerte faction also informed FIBA of the convening of the National Congress of the SBP to elect the national and regular officers of the group. In this election, Pangilinan et al. retained their respective positions.

51. Villafuerte and his block then filed a case before the RTC to invalidate the results of the election and recognize them as the legally elected officers of the SBP. This was granted. On appeal to the Court of Appeals, however, the decision was reversed. The Supreme Court likewise agreed with the appellate court and denied the petition, opining that:

> The membership validation resulted in the conferment of active membership status upon 19 BAP-SBP members, 17 of which participated in the June 12, 2008 meeting. Petitioners even constituted the majority of the Committee that undertook the task; they actively participated in the formulation of the validation rules based on the by-laws providing for this; some of them actively participated in the validation of the membership list and even voted along with other members of the Committee for the grant of active membership status to the 19 regular members. Thus, as correctly held by the Court of Appeals, petitioners are now estopped from assailing the validity and mandatory nature of the BAP-SBP's validation process as a prerequisite to a member's acquisition of active (voting) membership status.[107]

V. Philippine Amusement and Gaming Corporation

52. PAGCOR is a government-owned and controlled corporation tasked to regulate gambling in all forms in the Philippines. PAGCOR's Charter can be found in Presidential Decree No. 1869,[108] issued by the dictator Ferdinand Marcos. PAGCOR was formed in order to centralize all games of chance within one governmental regulatory body.[109]

107. *Villafuerte v. Moreno*, 617 Phil. 1011 (2009).
108. *See* Consolidating and Amending Presidential Decrees Nos. 1067-A, 1067-B, 1067-C, 1399 and 1632, Relative to the Franchise and Powers of the Philippine Amusement and Gaming Corporation (PAGCOR), Presidential Decree No. 1869 (1983).
109. *Ibid.*, tit. 1, §1.

53. To fulfill this goal, PAGCOR was granted a legislative franchise to "operate and license gambling casinos, gaming clubs and other similar recreation or amusement places, gambling pools ... " within the Philippines.[110] PAGCOR runs nine casino branches and thirty-two satellite casinos around the Philippines.[111]

54. PAGCOR's activities in the area of gambling have always been contentious. In 1991, the Supreme Court had the chance to determine whether PAGCOR's existence was contrary to morals and public policy. In *Basco v. PAGCOR*, the issue before the Supreme Court was whether President Corazon Aquino's policy of veering away from the monopolistic and crony economy which haunted the previous administration was put in jeopardy by the very existence of PAGCOR. The Supreme Court ruled in the negative, as it said that the Constitution itself does not prohibit monopolies and that this issue was beyond its ambit, being a policy issue better left to the legislature.[112]

55. Aside from running its own casinos, PAGCOR also issues regulations for gambling activities and grants licenses to gambling operations. Of particular interest in gaming law has been the proliferation of Philippine Offshore Gaming Operations (POGO). Offshore gaming has been defined as "the offering by a PAGCOR Licensee of authorized online games of chance or sporting events via the internet using a network and software or program, exclusively to offshore authorized players."[113] Note that POGOs must ensure that Filipino citizens, wherever situated in the world, and foreign nationals in the Philippines, do not access the online gaming portals.[114] PAGCOR likewise prohibits POGOs from accepting bets and paying of winnings within the Philippine territory.[115] In short, POGOs are similar to gambling call centers in the Philippines, which, ironically, exclude Filipinos from their revenue-making activities.

56. These strict measures in POGO activities and the regimented process to secure an Offshore Gaming License have not deterred the entry of POGOs into the Philippines. Recent years have seen the entry of Chinese companies establishing and running POGOs in the Philippines. This has caused a considerable influx of Chinese nationals and has led to a number of political, national security, economic,

---

110. An Act Further Amending Presidential Decree No. 1869, Otherwise Known as PAGCOR Charter, Republic Act No. 9487, §1 (2007).
111. Philippine Amusement and Gaming Corporation Staff, *Our Corporate Profile*, Philippine Amusement and Gaming Corporation, http://www.pagcor.ph/pagcor-corporate-profile.php.
112. *Basco v. Philippine Amusements and Gaming Corp.*, 274 Phil. 323 (1991).
113. Philippine Amusement and Gaming Corporation Staff, *Offshore Gaming Regulatory Manual*, Philippine Amusement and Gaming Corporation (Jul. 3, 2018) 4, http://www.pagcor.ph/regulatory/pdf/offshore/Offshore-Gaming-Regulatory-Manual.pdf.
114. *Ibid.*, reg. 2, §3.
115. *Ibid.*

and legal issues.[116] For various reasons, including the COVID-19 pandemic, POGOs have declined in number in the Philippines, with the government revenues from POGOs down 46% in 2021.[117]

116. Daxim L. Lucas, *Pagcor Imposes Moratorium on New POGO Licenses*, Philippine Daily Inquirer (Aug. 20, 2019), https://business.inquirer.net/277179/pagcor-imposes-moratorium-on-new-pogo-licenses.
117. Ben O. de Vera, *POGO Tax Take Drops 46 Percent to P3.91 Billion in 2021*, Philippine Daily Inquirer (Apr. 07, 2022), https://business.inquirer.net/345482/pogo-tax-take-drops-46-percent-to-p3-91-billion-in-2021.

Chapter 2. Public Regulation

§1. Structure of Government

57. The 1987 Philippine Constitution is the highest law of the land. Drafted, passed, and ratified after the People Power Revolution of 1986, the 1987 Philippine Constitution was a response to the corruption, cronyism, and rampant human rights violations that characterized the administration of the deposed dictator Ferdinand Marcos.[118] Subsequent administrations have sought to amend the Constitution, but it remains effective in the same form and substance to this date, notwithstanding calls for modernization and the removal of foreign ownership restrictions on certain businesses and industries.

58. The Philippines is a democratic and republican state.[119] Its republican characteristic stems from the fact that its government authority emanates from the people through representatives chosen by nationwide and local elections. It also possesses elements of direct democracy through constitutional provisions allowing for initiative and referendum.[120] The structure and form of its government is and has always been presidential.[121] And while the current Constitution and its previous iterations have been influenced deeply by the United States, the Philippines has veered away from a federal form of government. Instead, the Philippines opted for a unitary government. Its LGUs, like its provinces and cities, are granted local autonomy[122] but are still subject to the supervision of the President.[123]

59. Similar to the United States, the Philippines has three branches of government: the executive, legislative, and judiciary. Executive power is vested in the President, who is elected by popular vote every six years[124] and is exercised through his or her administrative agencies. As noted earlier, two of the main sports governing bodies of the Philippines, the PSC and GAB, are attached to the Office of the President. The heads of both the PSC and GAB are presidential appointees and serve at the pleasure of the President.

60. Legislative power lies in Congress, particularly the Senate and the House of Representatives.[125] Aside from the power to enact laws that directly affect sports,

118. *See* Cecilia Munoz-Palma, *Closing Remarks of the President of the Constitutional Commission at the Final Session*, Official Gazette (Oct. 15, 1986), https://www.officialgazette.gov.ph/1986/10/15/closing-remarks-of-the-president-of-the-constitutional-commission-at-the-final-session-october-15-1986/.
119. Phil. Const. Art. II, §1.
120. Phil. Const. Art. VI, §§1 & 32.
121. Joaquin G. Bernas S.J., *The 1987 Constitution of the Republic of the Philippines: A Commentary* 239 (2009).
122. Phil. Const. Art. X, §2.
123. Phil. Const. Art. X, §4.
124. Phil. Const. Art. VII, §§1 & 4.
125. Phil. Const. Art. VI, §1.

Congress also has the power of the purse by enacting the annual budget of the country. This also affects Philippine sports as it determines the budget of the PSC and sporting events like the SEA Games. The lack of appropriate public funding for Philippine sports is a constant complaint from stakeholders, especially national athletes who train in government-owned facilities which are outdated and dilapidated.

61. There are twenty-four senators who are elected at large and serve a term of six years.[126] There have been quite a few senators who find their roots in sports. Robert Jaworski, a Philippine basketball legend who played and coached in the PBA from the 1970s to 1990s, served in the Senate during 1998–2004. He ran for reelection but lost. Following in his footsteps is Joel Villanueva, a collegiate basketball player who is currently serving his 2016–2022 term as senator.

62. Of course, no one can argue that the senator with the most distinguished sports résumé, whether past or present, is world champion boxer, Manny Pacquiao. His success as a boxer has yet to translate to legislation though. True to form, his first pet bill focused on boxing, particularly providing safeguards for professional boxers, but the bill has yet to be passed to law, despite its introduction way back in 2016.[127] Aside from his lawmaking ability, his critics have also questioned Pacquiao's commitment to his job because of his low attendance on Senate session days.[128] In any case, Pacquiao's legislative career is secure for now, as his term expired in 2022. In the 2022 National Elections, Pacquiao ran for President but lost.

63. The House of Representatives is composed of district representatives, who are elected by their corresponding districts, and party-list representatives, who make up 20% of the entire House. Before his stint at the Senate, Manny Pacquiao served as a district representative of his wife's hometown of Sarangani for two consecutive terms during 2010–2016. In the final regular session of the sixteenth Congress, he attended just one session day; coincidentally, this period also overlapped with Pacquiao's training for his rematch with American boxer Timothy Bradley.[129]

64. Party lists were originally envisioned as a vehicle for representation of marginalized and underrepresented sectors of society, such as indigenous cultural communities, peasants, urban poor, and the youth. However, a recent Supreme Court decision has opened up the party-list system to practically anyone, including political parties.[130] This has caused an influx of groups vying for a seat in the House through the party-list system, including organizations that represent and advocate for sports and athletes. One such group, the Puwersa ng Bayaning Atleta, won two

126. Phil. Const. Art. VI, §§2 & 4.
127. Camille Elemia, *After 2 Years, Senate Finally OKs Manny Pacquiao's First Pet Bill on Boxing*, Rappler (Sep. 10, 2018), https://www.rappler.com/sports/by-sport/boxing-mma/211638-pacquiao-bill-philippine-boxing-commision-creation-gets-senate-approval.
128. Sherrie Ann Torres, *4 Senators Record Perfect Session Attendance*, ABS-CBN News (Jun. 5, 2018), https://news.abs-cbn.com/news/06/05/18/4-senators-record-perfect-session-attendance.
129. Mara Cepeda, *Pacquiao Top Absentee in Congress*, Rappler (Jul. 27, 2016), https://www.rappler.com/nation/140143-pacquiao-attendance-last-session-16th-congress.
130. *See Atong Paglaum, Inc. v. Commission on Elections*, 707 Phil. 454 (2013).

party-list seats in the 2016 elections. In 2016, the Puwersa ng Bayaning Atleta authored a bill to create a Philippine Department of Sports, but this has yet to be passed into law. In mid-2019, House Deputy Speaker, Mikee Romero, of the party-list 1 PACMAN passed a resolution questioning whether foreign student-athletes should be banned from participating in collegiate sports, citing the foreign student-athletes (who largely hail from Africa) were "[destroying] the beautiful game of basketball ... ."[131] Unsurprisingly, Romero's proposal caused quite a ruckus and was criticized by ex-collegiate players for being unfounded and unreasonable.

65. The judicial department rounds off the last branch of the government, with the Supreme Court and lower courts exercising judicial power. Under the Constitution, judicial power consists of two things. First is the duty of the court to settle controversies involving legally demandable and enforceable rights.[132] Second is the power to determine whether any branch or instrumentality of the government has overstepped its respective mandates and has gravely abused its discretion in excess (or lack) of jurisdiction.[133]

66. Unlike the Supreme Courts of other countries where jurisdiction is limited to special controversies or constitutional issues, the Philippine Supreme Court is the final arbiter of *all* legal disputes. Hence, the fifteen justices of the Supreme Court must be ready to rule on any and all justiciable controversy that has yet to be resolved by the lower courts. The diversity of issues that the Supreme Court can and has actually ruled on is vast. The constitutionality of laws, interpretations of loan contracts, tax assessments, simple ejection cases, murder, annulment of marriages, disbarment of erring lawyers, election cases—these cases all fall within the purview and jurisdiction of the Supreme Court.

67. Even if the Supreme Court casts a wide net on controversies that it will resolve, it has set a policy of refusing to resolve cases involving field-of-play calls. In deciding against the father of a soap box derby driver disqualified for lugging a half-pound bolt in his pocket to boost his speed, the Supreme Court in *Philippine Soap Box Derby v. Court of Appeals* stated:

> In an increasingly litigious society, the ramifications of courts' increasing intrusions into matters which ought to be settled by sports bodies are many. Encouraging the trend would ultimately pervert the yet untouched area of childhood sporting events. Unless a clear case is found for arbitrary and brazen violations or applications of sports rules by officials and sponsors themselves, and no such thing happened here, it is best for courts to prudently leave things where they are.[134]

131. From The Wires, *Mikee Romero Wants Bill Banning Foreign Players in College Leagues*, Spin.ph (Sep. 30, 2019), https://www.spin.ph/basketball/uaap-men/mikee-romero-files-bill-seeking-ban-on-foreign-players-in-college-leagues-a1373-20190930.
132. Phil. Const. Art. VIII, §1.
133. *Ibid.*
134. *Philippine Soap Box Derby, Inc. v. Court of Appeals*, 319 Phil. 714 (1995).

68. The Supreme Court's ruling is grounded on sound policy. It noted that if courts were to extend their judicial power to field-of-play calls, anarchy and chaos would ensue as "virtually every decision by an umpire, or referee or sports judge could be subject to question and every disqualification based on a clear-cut rule would be qualified by the presence or absence of good faith or bad faith, or the question of motive or intent."[135] The Court saw the absurdity of having judges decide on field-of-play controversies, saying "[s]pectators will then have to await the result of sporting events, not from rafters or from media, but from announcements made by judges through court personnel reading aloud legal decisions."[136]

69. The irony of the decision is that despite its well-founded and well-written litany on the value of keeping sports out of courts, the Supreme Court still went on to decide the case instead of dismissing it outright. In any event, the Supreme Court upheld the young racer's disqualification, ultimately finding that his father had given him a half-pound weight to keep in his pocket and that this extra weight was indeed a blatant violation of soap box derby rules. The Court went on to pin the blame on the young racer's father, even going as far as saying that the father acted in bad faith.[137]

§2. Fundamental Rights

70. The 1987 Constitution is also the source of fundamental rights, specifically the Bill of Rights enshrined in Article III of the Constitution. However, it must be noted that even without the Bill of Rights, the Philippines must still comply with its international obligations under the Universal Declaration of Human Rights and the International Covenant on Civil and Political Rights. The Supreme Court was explicit in this regard when it ruled on the protection afforded to an individual during the interregnum between the dictator Marcos' regime and restoration of democracy under President Corazon Aquino.[138]

71. As a basic rule, the Bill of Rights limits and binds the power of the government and colors its relationship with its constituents. It is and has been used to protect people from possible abuses of the government and other state actors. For abuses of political and civil rights by private entities, redress can be found in Article 32 of the Civil Code of the Philippines—a provision that incorporates the rights found in the Constitution into legislation that binds both public officers and private individuals. However, despite this distinction, the Supreme Court has applied the Bill of Rights to private actors.[139] This lax approach in transposing constitutional law doctrines to issues between private parties does have its benefits, though, especially for athletes whose civil and political rights have been infringed on; as it

135. *Ibid.*
136. *Ibid.*
137. *Ibid.*
138. *Republic v. Sandiganbayan*, 454 Phil. 504 (2003).
139. *See* Mickey Ingles, *Are You Sure You Want to Post That? Examining Student Social Media Use and Constitutional Rights*, 59 Ateneo L. J. 723 (2014).

stands, advocates for these athletes can hook their arguments on both the Constitution and the Civil Code, regardless of whether the perpetrator is a state actor or not.

I. Due Process

72. The first clause of Article III, Section I of the Constitution states that "no person shall be deprived of life, liberty or property without due process of law."[140] The order of the wording is deliberate, with rights affecting life and liberty (along with its iterations) given priority both in protection and preference over property rights.[141] The Supreme Court made this pronouncement as early as 1973 when it recognized "the primacy of human rights over property rights … ."[142]

73. Due process consists of substantive and procedural due process. In a nutshell, substantive due process prohibits arbitrary and abusive laws. Procedural due process relates to the procedure the government and its agencies must follow to enforce and apply laws.

74. In enacting laws and ordinances that relate to sports, Congress and legislative bodies of local governments must ensure that the law complies with substantive due process. The Supreme Court has devised a two-pronged test for this. First, the law must further a public interest.[143] Second, the means or methods used to achieve such interest are reasonable.[144] If a law fails in either respect, the Supreme Court will not hesitate to declare it unconstitutional. In 1988, the Court did just that when it struck down a city ordinance that mandated anyone selling admission tickets for movies, games, contests, and performances to offer these at half price to children between seven and twelve years of age.[145] The Court not only found the penal provisions of the ordinance appalling—anyone caught violating it faced up to six months in prison—but also failed to see the public interest involved and promoted by the ordinance.[146]

75. The legality of gambling has always been an issue in the Philippines, especially with the clamor of certain religious groups as to the immorality of the practice. Gambling critics have pointed to the pernicious effects of gambling and how the practice does not serve or further any public interest. However, the Supreme Court has been quick to note that "the morality of gambling is not a justiciable

140. Phil. Const. Art. III, §1.
141. *See Phil. Blooming Mills Employees Organization v. Phil. Blooming Mills Co., Inc.*, 151-A Phil. 656 (1973).
142. *Ibid.*
143. *Balacuit v. Court of First Instance of Agusan Del Norte and Butuan City, Br. II*, 246 Phil. 189 (1988).
144. *Ibid.*
145. *Ibid.*
146. *Ibid.*

issue."[147] The Constitution does not prohibit gambling, and Congress is left to its own devices on how to characterize gambling.[148] The legislative answer to the issue of gambling has been to allow and legalize certain forms of it through the establishment of the PAGCOR, a government-owned and controlled corporation mandated to regulate gambling nationwide.[149] Hence, when a city sought to block the construction of a PAGCOR casino within its city limits through an ordinance, the Court declared the ordinance invalid for contravening the will of the legislature.[150]

76. In terms of procedural due process, government agencies must follow a minimum standard in enforcing laws. At its essence, procedural due process requires that one be given the opportunity to be heard.[151] Hence, even if government agencies like GAB have the power to revoke professional sports licenses at any time,[152] one can imagine that the licensee must at least be given a chance to plead his case in order to comply with procedural due process.

77. Procedural due process has also been transplanted to the private sector through the Labor Code of the Philippines (Labor Code),[153] as employers must comply with requirements of notice and hearing when terminating an employee.[154] The specific requirements on termination are discussed more thoroughly in Articles 278–287 of the Labor Code.

II. Equal Protection of the Laws

78. The second clause of Article III, Section I guarantees that no person "shall be denied the equal protection of laws."[155] While this seems like a blanket disavowal of classification of any type or for any reason, it simply means that those who are similarly situated should likewise be similarly treated as to rights and responsibilities. The Supreme Court has allowed classifications, as long as these are based on substantial distinctions, are germane to the purpose of the law, applies to future conditions, and applies equally belonging to the same chosen class.[156] This fourfold test has been a staple in Philippine jurisprudence in settling equal protection issues.

79. In a 1991 Supreme Court case, American basketball coach, Tim Cone, sought solace from the equal protection clause when he questioned a Labor Code provision requiring non-resident aliens to secure an Alien Employment Permit

---

147. *Magtajas v. Pryce Properties Corp., Inc.*, 304 Phil. 428 (1994).
148. *Ibid.*
149. *Ibid.*
150. *Ibid.*
151. *See Shu v. Dee*, 734 Phil. 204 (2014).
152. Presidential Decree No. 871, §4.
153. Labor Code of the Philippines, Presidential Decree No. 442 (as amended) (1974).
154. *See Salaw v. National Labor Relations Commission*, G.R. No. 90786, 279 Phil. 8 (1991).
155. Phil. Const. Art. III, §1.
156. *See People v. Cayat*, 68 Phil. 12 (1939).

(AEP) before employment with a local company.[157] To secure an AEP for a potential non-resident alien-employee, an employer must first prove that there are no other persons in the Philippines who are competent, able, and willing to perform the services. In 1989, Cone was recruited to coach a professional basketball team. However, the Basketball Coaches Association of the Philippines (BCAP) caught wind of this and argued that there were other basketball coaches who were willing to take on Cone's coaching duties. On this ground, Cone's AEP was revoked. On appeal with the Supreme Court, Cone questioned the AEP itself, arguing that the permit only applied to non-resident aliens and not to resident aliens—a violation of the equal protection clause. Unfortunately for Cone, the Supreme Court ruled that the AEP requirement was valid, noting that there indeed were substantial distinctions between a resident alien and a non-resident alien.[158]

80. The NACBIA also raises an equal protection issue, particularly with its treatment of athletes with disabilities (AWDs).[159] Passed in 2015, the NACBIA provides monetary and cash incentives for athletes who bring home medals in international events like the Olympics, the Asian Games, and the SEA Games. The problem is, AWDs who win medals in counterpart events like the Paralympics, Asian Para Games, and ASEAN Para Games are entitled to only half of what their able-bodied counterparts would receive. For example, if a Filipino wins a gold medal in the Olympics, he or she is set to get PDP 10,000,000 in cash from the government. However, if a Filipino Paralympian wins a gold medal in the Paralympics, he or she is only entitled to PDP 5,000,000. The NACBIA will undoubtedly fail the fourfold test for reasonable classification, as there is clear discrimination against AWDs.

III. Free Speech

81. Free speech is also enshrined and protected under the Philippine Constitution, particularly under Article III, section 4 which guarantees that "no law shall be passed abridging the freedom of speech, of expression, or of the press." Save for well-defined exceptions, the free speech clause prohibits both prior restraint, or official action that restricts speech in advance of publication, and subsequent punishment, or any action that sanctions speech after publication.

82. The protection afforded to speech has been interpreted to include symbolic speech. This is an important consideration for athletes who wish to follow in the footsteps of American athlete Colin Kaepernick and protest governmental action by engaging in actions that implicate free speech, such as kneeling during the national anthem. Interestingly, the Supreme Court has dealt with a similar situation in *Ebranilag v. the Division Superintendent of Schools of Cebu.*[160] In the said case, elementary students—members of the Jehovah's Witnesses, a religious community that

157. *General Milling Corp. v. Torres*, 273 Phil. 434 (1991).
158. *Ibid.*
159. National Athletes and Coaches Benefits and Incentives Act, §3(c).
160. *Ebranilag v. Division Superintendent of Schools of Cebu*, 321 Phil. 966 (1995).

strictly prohibits idolatry—were expelled for refusing to salute the flag during the school's flag ceremony.[161] While the case was decided in favor of the students mostly based on freedom of religion principles, the Concurring Opinion of Justice Isagani Cruz still recognized that free speech includes the right to stay silent.[162] The Court noted that the students were not disrupting any school activities, as they stood quietly while everyone else sang the national anthem and saluted the flag. Whether the same principles can or will be applied to an athlete who peacefully and quietly refuses to salute the flag remains to be seen, especially since protesting athletes might not have freedom of religion as an additional argument for support.

83. Another challenge for the protesting athlete in terms of free speech is the Flag and Heraldic Code of the Philippines (Flag Code).[163] Passed in 1998, the Flag Code was passed to inculcate reverence and respect for the flag and national anthem in all Filipinos. The Flag Code states that whenever the Philippine national anthem is played at a public gathering, the attending public should stand at attention and sing it.[164] The law actually requires that the "singing must be done with fervor."[165]

84. Under the Flag Code, athletes who choose to protest and kneel during the national anthem face criminal charges. He or she can be penalized by public censure which will be published at least once in a newspaper of general circulation.[166] And worse, the protesting athlete can also face jail time for not more than a year and/or pay a fine of not more than PDP 20,000.[167] While the Flag Code raises constitutional issues, especially in light of *Ebranilag*, its constitutionality has yet to be challenged in front of the Supreme Court. In fact, the Flag Code saw application fairly recently when thirty-four moviegoers were arrested for not standing during the national anthem prior to the exhibition of a popular Filipino movie.[168] One can imagine a similar fate awaits athletes who wish to take a stand by refusing to stand during a sports event.

85. Unlike symbolic speech, libel finds no protection under the Philippine Constitution. In fact, libel is criminalized under the Revised Penal Code (RPC) and can be a welcome safeguard for athletes who may find disparaging remarks written about them in the sports pages of newspapers. Libel is defined as a "public and malicious imputation of a crime, or a vice or defect, real or imaginary, or any act, omission, condition, status, or circumstance tending to cause the dishonor, discredit or contempt a natural or juridical person, or to blacken he memory of one who is

---

161. *Ibid.*
162. *Ibid.* (Cruz, J., concurring).
163. Flag and Heraldic Code of the Philippines, Republic Act No. 8491 (1998).
164. *Ibid.*, §38.
165. *Ibid.*
166. *Ibid.*, §48.
167. *Ibid.*, §50.
168. Arnell Ozaeta, *34 Moviegoers Arrested for Not Standing Up to Sing "Lupang Hinirang" Inside Cinema*, The Philippine Star (Sep. 6, 2018), https://www.philstar.com/nation/2018/09/06/1849213/34-moviegoers-arrested-not-standing-sing-lupang-hinirang-inside-cinema.

dead."[169] In 2014, the Supreme Court affirmed that libel can also now be committed through the internet when it ruled on the validity of the Cybercrime Prevention Act of 2012.[170]

86. Regardless of *how* libel is committed, one important element must be considered in actions of libel: the existence of malice. The burden of proving malice will, in turn, depend on whether the victim may be considered a public figure or not. Public figures who wish to recover from libelous statements must prove that such statements were tainted actual malice, or that these were made with reckless disregard of the truth.[171] If the victim is not a public figure, then malice is presumed, and the burden shifts to the accused.[172] This begs the question of whether an athlete or sports personality can be considered a public figure for purposes of libel.

87. The Supreme Court has considered the following as public figures: "public officers, famous inventors and explorers, war heroes and even ordinary soldiers, an infant prodigy ... ."[173] However, it has yet to determine the threshold an athlete or sports personality must cross to be considered a public figure. The case may turn on this issue alone. It is easy to imagine a local court tacking the label of "public figure" to popular athletes, such as a professional basketball player, a world champion boxer like Manny Pacquiao, or an Olympic medalist. But what about other athletes who do not reach the same level of fame and popularity, such as student-athletes or medalists in other international competitions like the SEA Games. Will they be considered public figures as well? Until a case of libel against an athlete reaches the Supreme Court, lawyers are free to advocate on either side of the fence on a case-to-case basis.

88. Schools and universities must also consider free speech implications if and when they decide to impose social media policies on their student-athletes. In a country like the Philippines where social media use is prevalent and student-athletes rival professional athletes in popularity and marketability, some schools have adopted social media policies to help their student-athletes navigate the precarious world of posts and tweets.

89. A kneejerk reaction to social media policies revolve around arguments on prior restraint, which is understandable, given that these policies outline what student-athletes can and cannot post online. However, the Supreme Court has recognized the power of schools to regulate speech because of their special duty and role in shaping the youth. Hence, schools can regulate certain constitutional rights, such as free speech, because they cannot mold young minds without the power to restrict or discipline.

---

169. The Revised Penal Code, Act No. 3815, Art. 353 (1932).
170. *See Disini, Jr. v. Secretary of Justice*, 727 Phil. 28 (2014).
171. *Lopez v. Court of Appeals*, 145 Phil. 219 (1970).
172. The Revised Penal Code, Arts. 354 & 361.
173. *Ayer Productions Pty. Ltd. v. Capulong*, 243 Phil. 1007 (1988).

90. Of course, the power of schools to do so can only be exercised to a certain extent, lest they go overboard and unduly restrict the rights of their student-athletes to speak. To make sure that these policies remain constitutional and valid, American and Philippine jurisprudence have given some helpful boundaries for schools and universities (note that the Philippine Supreme Court looks to American cases as persuasive authority in interpreting shared constitutional provisions, such as the free speech clause).[174]

91. First, social media policy must only refer to on-campus speech. Schools can only regulate, restrict, or discipline student-athletes' speech if the speech was made on campus. Schools can regulate on-campus speech more than off-campus speech because of the special role of schools in shaping the youth. However, once outside the school setting, the schools somewhat lose the power to regulate because the student-athletes' right to free speech receives the same protection as any other citizen. As such, it is important to determine what constitutes on-campus speech.

92. American and Philippine cases have considered the following on-campus speech: first, when the speech is made during a school-sanctioned event;[175] second, when, regardless of its geographic origin, it causes (or foreseeably causes) substantial disruption of school activities;[176] and third, when, *even* if it was made physically outside of campus, there is sufficient nexus or connection between the social media post and the school.[177] Note the third iteration of on-campus speech; the posts do not have to be uploaded within the geographic confines of the campus. As long as it causes disrupts schoolwork or can be connected to the school, it can be considered on-campus speech and, therefore, subject to discipline or regulation.

93. The social media policy can also impose restrictions on the following speech, which are constitutionally unprotected in the first place: vulgar and lewd speech;[178] speech that promotes illegal drug use;[179] and obscene and libelous speech. The policy may also refer to or incorporate the rules and guidelines of the student manual or handbook.[180] Hence, if the school handbook has strict rules against alcohol intake and nudity or sexually suggestive behavior, a social media policy prohibiting student-athletes from posting photos and videos of them binge drinking or posing suggestively in swimwear is arguably valid and constitutional.

---

174. *See*, e.g., *Gonzalez v. Katigbak*, 222 Phil. 225 (1985) & *Pita v. Court of Appeals*, 258-A Phil. 134 (1989).
175. *Morse v. Frederick*, 551 U.S 393 (2007).
176. *J.C. v. Beverly Hills*, 711 F.Supp. 2d 1094 (9th Cir. 2010).
177. *Ibid.*
178. *Bethel School District v. Fraser*, 478 U.S. 675 (1986).
179. *Morse*, 551 U.S. 393.
180. *Vivares v. St. Theresa's College*, 744 Phil. 451 (2014).

IV. Right to Privacy

94. Discipline and restrictions on social media also raise the issue of an individual's right to privacy. The Supreme Court has stated that the right to privacy mainly consists of three aspects: locational or situational privacy, informational privacy, and decisional privacy.[181] Among the three, informational privacy, or the right of individuals to control information about themselves, is relevant in social media issues.[182]

95. In terms of social media, the extent of one's right to informational privacy depends on the user's reasonable expectation of privacy, which, in turn, is largely determined by his or her privacy settings.[183] In a case where a private high school sanctioned students who uploaded suggestive photos on Facebook, the Supreme Court expounded on the nature of Facebook as a tool for social interaction. As "public" was the default setting for sharing photos on Facebook, it was up to the students to show that they had a reasonable expectation of privacy. The Court found that while the students' photos were viewable by "friends only," it did not indicate that the students had a reasonable expectation of privacy, as non-friends can still access and see these photos through Facebook's tagging system.[184] Schools and universities must consider this privacy angle in crafting their social media policies to avoid infringing on student-athletes' privacy rights.

96. Mandatory drug testing for student-athletes also raises privacy concerns. In 2008, the Supreme Court was tasked to determine if drug testing in secondary and tertiary schools violates the right to privacy.[185] Looking to American jurisprudence for guidance, the Supreme Court noted the duty of schools to protect the health and well-being of their students because they stand *in loco parentis*. As such, mandatory drug testing of students was declared constitutional as long as these tests were random and devoid of suspicion.[186] As an interesting aside, the Supreme Court used the American case of *Vernonia School District 47J v. Acton*[187] as a basis for the decision. Those familiar with Vernonia will remember that the case upheld the constitutionality of random drug testing for student-athletes.

97. In terms of drug testing for and the right of privacy of athletes in the private sector, the Supreme Court has likewise given its stamp of constitutionality, as long as the drug testing is random and devoid of suspicion.[188] If it was the duty of schools that was the determinative factor in mandatory drug testing for students, it was the lesser expectation of privacy of employees that was the anchor for drug testing in

---

181. *Ibid.*
182. *Ibid.*
183. *Ibid.*
184. *Ibid.*
185. *Social Justice Society v. Dangerous Drugs Board*, 591 Phil. 393 (2008).
186. *Ibid.*
187. *Vernonia School District 47J v. Acton*, 515 U.S. 646 (1995).
188. *Social Justice Society*, 591 Phil. 393.

the workplace.[189] The Court noted that employees' privacy interest in offices and the workplace was considerably reduced because of work policies and management prerogative. Hence, mandatory, random, and suspicionless drug testing was a reasonable and constitutional intrusion on an employee's privacy.[190] The same reduced expectation of privacy is also present in sports teams—if not even less given the practice of common undress in locker rooms and showers.

V. Freedom of Religion

98. Article III, section 5 of the Constitution deals with religion, specifically stating that "No law shall be made respecting an establishment of religion, or prohibiting the free exercise thereof. The free exercise and enjoyment of religious profession and worship, without discrimination or preference, shall forever be allowed."[191] The provision covers two clauses. The first clause is the non-establishment clause, which, at its simplest, prohibits state advancement or endorsement of a particular religion. The second clause is the free exercise clause, which allows citizens to believe whatever they want to believe with the caveat that the state may restrict this freedom if there is a compelling state interest it wishes to further use the least intrusive means possible.[192]

99. As a predominantly Catholic country, the Philippines has found this constitutionally mandated separation of church and state easier said than done. While the Supreme Court has adopted the approach of benevolent neutrality in order to accommodate all religions and excuse conscientious objectors to certain government regulations,[193] the truth is, Catholic traditions permeate deep into almost every aspect of Filipino life, sports included. For example, varsity teams of Philippine public schools or universities regularly start training sessions and games with a prayer—a violation of the non-establishment clause under American jurisprudence.[194] A necessary consequence of these pregame religious traditions and rituals is the inclusion of non-Catholics or non-Christians, who may feel compelled to join out of a sense of obligation to the team—a violation of the free exercise clause.

100. This aspect of an athlete's fundamental rights is often glossed over, particularly because complaints have been few and far between due to the homogeneity of the country's religious beliefs. However innocuous this issue seems to be, sports stakeholders must take this into consideration to avoid any future litigation borne out of non-accommodation. To be specific, state actors, such as public schools and universities, would do well to protect the religious rights of their athletes, whatever religion or sect they belong to, because, in the end, the protection of a single person's rights is the protection of everyone's rights.

189. *Ibid.*
190. *Ibid.*
191. Phil. Const. Art. III, §5.
192. *Estrada v. Escritor*, 455 Phil. 411 (2003).
193. *Ibid.*
194. *Santa Fe Independent School Dist. v. Doe*, 530 U.S. 290 (2000).

VI. Right to Travel

101. The Constitution likewise protects the right to travel, stating that it shall not be impaired, "except in the interest of national security, public safety, or public health, as may be provided by law."[195] While anyone who has a Philippine passport may potentially travel abroad, traveling with Filipino children below eighteen years of age comes with the additional requirement of a government travel clearance. Filipino children below eighteen who wish to travel abroad with someone other than their parent or parents need a travel clearance from the Department of Social Welfare and Development (DSWD) before leaving the country.[196]

102. Applying for the DSWD travel clearance requires the submission of documents, one of which is the written consent to travel issued by both parents (or the single parent, as the case may be), to the nearest DSWD Field Office.[197] The travel clearance is valid for a year.[198]

103. Note, however, that the travel clearance is not required when the minor travels with either parent or his or her guardian.[199] A minor who is not Filipino and holds a foreign passport also does not need the DSWD travel clearance.[200]

104. The DSWD travel clearance is particularly relevant and important to owners and managers of youth sports teams and academies who seek to train abroad. Youth national teams participating in tournaments abroad must also consider this additional requirement, as it actually carries penal implications. Traveling without the required DSWD clearance is a crime, with the perpetrator facing fifteen years in jail for attempted trafficking in persons.[201]

VII. Eminent Domain and Just Compensation

105. Among the three inherent powers of the government, the power of eminent domain is limited by two important constitutional requirements: the taking must be for public use and be justly compensated.[202] The government must take these two considerations to heart, especially when it seeks to build sports facilities and infrastructure in a private property. Negotiations with the property owner normally precede the taking of property, but if these fall through, the government must resort to the power of eminent domain.

---

195. Phil. Const. Art. III, §6.
196. Department of Social Welfare and Development Staff, *Frequently Asked Questions (FAQs)—Clearance for Minors Travelling Abroad*, http://www.dswd.gov.ph/frequently-ask-questions-faqs/.
197. *Ibid.*
198. *Ibid.*
199. *Ibid.*
200. *Ibid.*
201. Anti-Trafficking in Persons Act of 2003, Republic Act No. 9208 (as amended), §4-A (2003).
202. Phil. Const. Art. III, §9.

122. Negligence is the "failure to observe for the protection of the interests of another person, that degree of care, precaution and vigilance which the circumstances justly demand."[230] The current test of negligence is as follows:

> Conduct is said to be negligent when a prudent man in the position of the tortfeasor would have foreseen that an effect harmful to another was sufficiently probable to warrant his foregoing the conduct or guarding against its consequences.[231]

123. Negligence greatly depends on foreseeability. If the risk is unforeseeable, then one cannot be considered negligent. Also, negligence is a relative term, and the existence thereof is judged by the surrounding circumstances.[232] Hence, the act of one in a certain situation may be called negligent, while the same act in another situation may not be called such.

124. Negligence-based actions can be trumped by the defense of the assumption of risk, making a recovery for injuries sustained during sports competitions difficult. The assumption of risk has been recognized as a viable defense in personal injury cases[233] and is defined as the "voluntary assumption of a risk of harm arising from the negligent conduct of the defendant. It presupposes an intentional exposure to a known peril."[234]

125. The defense first reared its head in Philippine jurisprudence in 1949, in a classic case of animals not understanding the old adage of not biting the hand that feeds them. In *Afialda v. Hisole,*[235] a water buffalo gored to death the man who was tasked to take care of it.[236] The Court ruled against the sister of the caretaker in a case for damages and stated that "being injured by the animal under those circumstances was one of the risks of the occupation which he had voluntarily assumed and for which he must take the consequences."[237]

126. In sports-related injuries, defendants—learning from the triumphant water buffalo in *Afialda*—can easily argue that the injured player assumed the risk of an injury by participating in a sports competition. After all, injuries are foreseeable risks in sports.[238] Basketball players land awkwardly going for a rebound and twist their ankles. Soccer players assume the risk of bruises and bloody shins from all the tackles they have to endure on the field. These are all part of the game, risks that the players can reasonably foresee and are, therefore, difficult to mount an action on.

230. *Barias*, 23 Phil 434 at 437.
231. *Picart v. Smith*, 37 Phil. 809 (1918).
232. Pineda, *supra* note 219, at 8.
233. *Afialda v. Hisole*, 85 Phil. 67 (1949).
234. Pineda, *supra* note 219, at 74.
235. *Afialda*, 85 Phil 67.
236. *Ibid.*
237. *Ibid.*, at 69.
238. Glenn Wong, *Essentials of Amateur Sports Law*, 412 (1994).

127. The same result of non-recovery can be said of actions based on intentional torts, albeit for a different reason. Note that the current state of Philippine jurisprudence includes intentional acts within the application of Article 2176.[239] Article 2176 makes it clear that intentional acts are included in the scope of torts, as the damage may have occurred either through "fault or negligence."[240] The former implies the presence of intent. Fault has also been defined to be the "execution of a positive act but the act was done contrary to the normal way of doing it and ultimately causing damage or injury to another."[241]

128. The problem with actions based on intentional torts is the difficulty of proving intent. In cases where the intent to harm is obvious—such as when a basketball player punches an opposing player straight on in the face and then dances afterward to celebrate the blow—then the case can most certainly flourish. But what about cases where the intent of the defendant is not readily apparent? Intent is difficult to prove in sports, given the competitive nature and the repeated clashing of bodies in contact sports.

129. The answer lies in adopting the duty of care in the United States, which mandates athletes to refrain from the reckless acts which disregard safety rules or the safety of their co-participants.[242] The standard serves as a good middle ground between negligence and intentional torts that allows athletes to recover from injuries sustained during sports events. It does not douse the competitive spirit and vigor of sports because it still allows room for a fair amount of negligence to be overcome by the assumption of risk,[243] but at the same time, it does not condone intentional injurious acts which have no place in sports, to begin with.

130. Adopting the American standard is legally possible in the Philippines, as American and Philippine torts share the same foundations and principles. First, as noted earlier, Philippine law allows different standards of duty depending on the situation. A standard of care specific and focused on participant-on-participant injuries fits nicely into the Philippine legal framework for torts.

131. Second, the Supreme Court recognizes the importance of the connection between rules and the injuries or situations that they seek to prevent. A 1973 decision has already alluded to the legal duty to abide by safety rules. In *Teague v. Fernandez,*[244] the Supreme Court held the defendant liable for violating a safety ordinance that caused overcrowding and subsequent injuries to some students.[245] The Court held her liable because "the accident ... was the very thing which the ... ordinance [would have prevented.]."[246]

239. Pineda, *supra* note 219, at 5.
240. Civil Code of the Philippines, Art. 2176.
241. Pineda, *supra* note 219, at 8.
242. *Nabozny*, 31 Ill. App. 3d 212.
243. *Jaworski v. Kiernan,* 241 Conn. 399, 410 (Conn. 1997).
244. *Teague v. Fernandez*, 151 Phil. 648 (1973).
245. *Ibid.*
246. *Ibid.*

requisites are met.[272] First, the person waiving his or her right must actually have that right.[273] Second, the person must have the legal capacity to give up the said right.[274] Third, the waiver must be clear and unequivocal.[275]Finally, the waiver should not be contrary to law, morals, public order, public policy, or prejudicial to a third person.[276]

146. As promising as waivers sound, waivers only protect organizers and facility owners from acts of negligence. Under Philippine law, waivers for actions based on future fraud are void.[277]Likewise, waivers for actions based on gross negligence are void, as these are contrary to public policy.[278] Gross negligence implies an absence or failure to exercise even the slightest care or diligence.[279] Hence, it would be quite difficult for a gym owner to use a waiver to protect itself from liability from, say, letting its patrons use faulty gym equipment without warning or notice.

147. In terms of organizer liability, the seminal case is *Abrogar v. Cosmos Bottling Company* decided by the Supreme Court in 2017.[280] *Abrogar* involved the tragic death of Rommel Abrogar, a minor, in 1980 in a junior marathon organized by Intergames, Inc. A jeepney fatally struck Abrogar as he was running the ten-kilometer race in Quezon City, Metro Manila. Abrogar's parents sued Cosmos Bottling Company, the sponsor of the race, and Intergames, Inc., the organizer. The case revolved around whether Intergames, Inc. was negligent in organizing the race and if their negligence was the proximate cause of Abrogar's death.

148. In its defense, Intergames, Inc. pointed to the jeepney driver for Abrogar's death. The organizer also stated that they exercised due diligence in the conduct of the race by implementing safety and precautionary measures to protect the runners. Intergames, Inc. argued that it did all it could to keep participants safe. According to Intergames, Inc., the blame should land squarely on the jeepney driver who ran over Abrogar.

149. The Supreme Court ruled against Intergames, Inc. It found not only the organizer negligent in conducting the race but also the proximate cause of Abrogar's death. As to the negligence in conducting and organizing the marathon, the Supreme Court found that Intergames' safeguards were inadequate. Noting that the standard of diligence is determined by the persons, time, and place, the Court stated that a higher degree of diligence was required because the participants were minors and teenagers.

---

272. *Intestate Estate of the Late Borromeo v. Borromeo*, 236 Phil. 184 (1987).
273. *Ibid.*
274. *Ibid.*
275. *Ibid.*
276. *Ibid.*
277. Civil Code of the Philippines, Art. 1171.
278. Edgardo L. Paras, *Civil Code of the Philippines Annotated* 140 (2008).
279. *Amedo v. Rio y Olabarrieta, Inc.*, 95 Phil. 33 (1954).
280. *Abrogar v. Cosmos Bottling Co.*, 807 Phil. 317 (2017).

150. First, local authorities informed Intergames, Inc. beforehand that roads would not be closed for the event. However, Intergames, Inc. still chose to push through with the event, knowing full well that kids would be running alongside moving vehicles. The Court even noted that the organizer had no obligation to have the race in Quezon City. They could have held the race elsewhere, preferably in a city or municipality where the roads would have been closed to accommodate the race.

151. Second, Intergames, Inc. did not manage the race route properly. The organizers did not have their own employees or personnel to deploy for safety purposes. Instead, they relied on volunteers (some of which were young boy scouts) to ensure the safety of the runners. The volunteer crew, the Court found, was not properly instructed on their duties and respective tasks to protect the young runners from any unfortunate accidents. The lack of coordination between the organizers and the volunteers *and* the lack of volunteers itself placed runners in a dangerous situation.

152. On the issue of proximate cause, the Supreme Court found that it was Intergames, Inc.'s negligence which was the proximate cause of Abrogar's death—even if it was the jeepney driver who dealt the fatal blow to the young runner. Proximate cause has been defined as "that which, in natural and continuous sequence, unbroken by any new cause, produces an event, and without which the event would not have occurred."[281] Intergames, Inc.'s defense revolved around the argument that the jeepney driver was an efficient intervening cause that broke the "natural and continuous sequence" which led to Abrogar's death.

153. Despite the strong argument of Intergames, Inc., the Supreme Court still pinned proximate cause on Intergames, Inc. for a number of reasons. First, Intergames, Inc.'s negligence set the stage for Abrogar's death. Second, the organizer knew that an accident of this nature could happen. It was foreseeable, an avoidable risk which could have been avoided by conducting the race in another city with blocked-off roads or by having adequate personnel deployed around the route. Finally, the negligence of the jeepney driver was not sufficient to break the natural course of events that began with Intergames, Inc.'s negligence and ended with Abrogar's death. It was not a recognized efficient intervening cause because a vehicle hitting a runner on an open road was foreseeable to begin with.

154. Unsurprisingly, Intergames, Inc. also raised the defense of assumption of risk. It claimed that Abrogar knew the risks of running a mini-marathon and still chose to go through with it. The Supreme Court dismissed this argument quickly, stating that being struck by a vehicle while running a marathon was not a foreseeable risk one could assume.

155. Intergames, Inc. also presented the waiver Abrogar had signed before running. However, the Supreme Court found this waiver ineffective, considering it was

281. *Ibid.*

signed by a minor and finding that a minor could not comprehend the risk involved in the race, especially an unforeseeable risk of getting struck by a car.

156. *Abrogar* is a good case that now sets the duty of care for organizers into jurisprudence. It is a timely case as well, as marathons, triathlons, and ironman races are regularly conducted in the Philippines. Sadly, some of these races have seen untimely deaths of their participants. In 2017, a triathlete died because of cardiac arrest during the swim leg of an ironman event in Cebu.[282] A participant suffered a similar sad fate in 2009 during an event in Camarines Sur.[283] And more recently, a college student collapsed and died during a qualifying run for a university-based mountaineering organization.[284] Hopefully, young Abrogar's death could serve as a beacon for safety in upcoming events and races.

§5. Criminal Liability

I. Revised Penal Code

157. The general criminal law for the Philippines can be found in the RPC. Passed in 1930, the RPC borrows heavily from the Spanish criminal code.[285] While the RPC has seen its fair amount of amendments and survived an equal amount of criticism, it has survived the test of time and continues to serve as the main legal reference for criminal laws. The RPC outlines the basic criminal law system of the country and various criminal offenses in its 365 or so articles. Most RPC-based crimes need criminal intent to prosecute, but it also criminalizes certain negligent acts.[286] A number of these can and have actually been applied in the sports context.

158. Participant-on-participant injuries cannot only lead to a suit for damages under tort law but can also see the guilty party spend a considerable amount of time in jail. If the injury is coupled with an intent to harm (such as an intentional tort), then a crime of physical injuries can be slapped on the offending party. The actual nomenclature of the crime and the corresponding penalties will depend on the severity of the injury. If the victim becomes insane or impotent or loses an eye, hand, or leg, or is incapable of working for more than thirty days, then a crime of serious physical injuries has been committed.[287] If there are injuries but considerably less

282. SunStar Philippines Staff, *Triathlete Dies in Ironman's Swim Leg*, SunStar Philippines (Aug. 7, 2017), https://www.sunstar.com.ph/article/157164.
283. Spot.ph Staff, *Updated: Executive, 52, Dies in Ironman 70.3 Triathlon in Cam Sur*, Spot.ph (Aug. 23, 2009), https://www.spot.ph/newsfeatures/29497/executive-drownin-cwc-ironman-in-cam-sur.
284. Margarita C. Gonzalez & Thea Unson, *LM, OSA to Improve Safety Measures after Undergraduate Student's Passing*, The Guidon (Oct. 20, 2018), http://www.theguidon.com/1112/main/2018/10/lm-osa-improve-safety-measures-undergraduate-students-passing/.
285. *See*, e.g., *People v. Formigones*, 87 Phil. 658 (1950) & *Tanega v. Masakayan*, 125 Phil. 966 (1967).
286. The Revised Penal Code, Art. 3.
287. *Ibid.*, Art. 263.

than those for serious physical injuries, the accused faces a charge of either less serious physical injuries or slight physical injuries, again depending on the severity of the damage.[288] Finally, if there was no intent (such as when the act was coupled with recklessness), but the injuries were considerable, the offending party can still be charged with reckless imprudence.[289]

159. As emotions may sometimes reach fever levels, players and participants might find the referees and officials caught in the crosshairs of their ire. There have been incidents where players have laid a hand or two on a referee in the Philippines, whether intentionally or simply, to get past an official who was blocking the path of another player.[290] The question remains, however, if this constitutes direct assault under the RPC. A direct assault is committed when any person employs force or intimidation or even attacks a person in authority or his or her agents.[291] Is a referee considered a person in authority under the RPC then?

160. For purposes of direct assault, the following are considered persons in authority or an agent of a person in authority: persons directly vested with the jurisdiction (such as a member of a judicial court or governmental body), persons charged with maintaining public order and protection of security of life and property, and teachers, professors and persons charged with the supervisions of schools.[292] As can be seen, a referee or a sports official, while holding some sort of authority over the sport or match in question, is not a person in authority for purposes of direct assault. Of course, this does not preclude a case of direct assault if the referee or official falls within one of the groups enumerated, such as when a teacher moonlights as a referee during a school intramural game.

161. Speaking of referees, the zebra-clothed officials are also the subject of ire from fans. Often, fans shout things at referees, opposing players, and even players from their own team that they would not dare say face-to-face. These slurs *may* cross the line into unprotected speech, especially if they constitute the crime of slander. Slander is criminalized under the RPC as oral defamation, a version of libel. Libel is a crime on its own, defined as "a public and malicious imputation of a crime, or of a vice or defect, real or imaginary, or any act, omission, condition, status, or circumstance tending to cause the dishonor, discredit or contempt of a natural or juridical person, or to blacken the memory of one who is dead."[293]

162. To carry a conviction of libel and slander, the following elements must be present: the allegation of a discreditable act or condition, the publication of the charge, the identity of the defamed must be identified, and the allegation must be

288. The Revised Penal Code, Arts. 265 & 266.
289. *Ibid.*, Art. 365.
290. Aimee Grace Tapeceria, *PBA || Ref Edward Aquino and Calvin Abueva Incident || Alaska v. Barako || 02/17/13*, at 00:03-0:23 (Feb. 18, 2013), https://www.youtube.com/watch?v=LhVJEVC-E9g.
291. The Revised Penal Code, Art. 148.
292. *Ibid.*, Art. 152.
293. *Ibid.*, Art. 353.

made with malice. In a classic sports example, a fan may shout that a referee has been paid off by another team to the detriment of the fan's team, presumably losing because of a bad call or two.

163. The first, second and third elements are easily satisfied. While yet undecided by the Supreme Court, it seems alleging that a referee being paid off by an opposing team causes dishonor to the referee—it is logical to conclude so, given that a referee's job and reputation are determined by his or her fairness and impartiality. The shout of an impassioned fan is enough to satisfy the element of publication. As the referee is easily identifiable, the third element of identification is also satisfied.[294]

164. As to the fourth element of malice, the threshold question is whether referees are public figures. This is important because it determines if the presumption of malice applies. Simply put, a public figure is a celebrity, someone whose accomplishments or fame has given the public a legitimate interest in one's life.[295] A public figure also includes a private person involved in a matter of public or general interest.

165. Every defamatory imputation is presumed to be malicious if no good intention or justifiable motive for it is shown.[296] However, this presumption does not apply when the subject of defamation is a public figure. If the object of the defamatory remark is a public figure, actual malice on the part of the defaming party must be shown.[297] Actual malice means the offender made the defamatory statement with the knowledge that it was false or with reckless disregard of its falsity, with the latter standard requiring a "high degree of awareness of probable falsity," a rule transposed from American jurisprudence.[298]

166. It would seem farfetched to consider any Filipino referee a public figure, except if that referee was boxing referee, Carlos Padilla, Jr., who had the privilege of sharing the ring with Muhammad Ali and Joe Frazier for Thrilla in Manila. As an aside, Carlos Padilla was a public figure, to begin with (as he was a movie star before he became a boxing referee) and retained his celebrity status as an endorser and the face of a local rubbing alcohol brand.

167. The public figure quandary is relevant to defamatory remarks against athletes. Are athletes public figures? An American court has implied that athletes can be considered public figures by entering an activity which "society [has chosen] to direct massive public attention to ... ."[299] Whether Philippine courts will extend

---

294. Of course, a defense attorney can raise the argument that in games with more than one referees (like basketball), the defamed official is not easily identifiable.
295. *Ayer Productions Pty. Ltd.*, 243 Phil. 1007.
296. The Revised Penal Code, Art. 354.
297. *New York Times Co. v. Sullivan*, 376 U.S. 254 (1964).
298. *Disini, Jr.*, 727 Phil. 28.
299. *Chuy v. Philadelphia Eagles Football Club*, 431 F. Supp. 254 (E.D. Pa. 1977).

these to local athletes remains to be seen. It will be interesting how courts will consider student-athletes, given that student-athletes are often more popular than their professional counterparts.

168. Another crime relating to student-athletes and amateurs is the falsification of public documents. With age restrictions being a condition for eligibility, some teams engage in the dubious practice of skimming a few years off their players' ages. A classic and sad example of this was the Philippine Little League team that participated in the Little League World Cup in Pennsylvania, the USA in 1992. Apparently, the Philippines fielded a team of overage players—the catcher in particular looking too senior to be 12 years old—by submitting fake documents and outright lying about the ages of the players.[300] If these documents were birth certificates or passports, then the crime of falsification of public documents had been committed.[301] A claim that the documents were for private use only, such as entry forms to a tournament, does not relieve the person of any criminal liability; the falsification of private documents is also criminalized, as long as there was an intent to damage a third party.[302] It would be interesting for a court to determine if having an unfair advantage in a sporting event can constitute an intent to damage under the law.

169. Corruption is a word often thrown around as one of the reasons why Philippine sports is not as developed as it should be. Ask anyone why the Philippines has only one Olympic gold, and the answer would most likely be mismanagement by government and federation officials. For example, before she won the country's only Olympic gold in history during Tokyo 2020, Hidilyn Diaz went to social media pleading for financial support to continue her dream to compete in the Olympics, prompting journalists to ask: where does all the funding go?[303] Sadly, the answer is often a *who* rather than a *where*. Greedy sports officials who pocket public funds earmarked for sports face the crime of malversation of public funds or property.[304] Note that the PSC allocates and distributes public funds to eligible NSAs for the development of their respective sports. If the culprits are NSA officials, they may still be held liable for malversation, even if they are private persons, as the crime includes private individuals who are given charge of public funds.[305]

170. Sexual abuse in sports has also reared its ugly head in the Philippine context. In 2017, an arrest warrant was issued against a volleyball coach who would sneak out his player—who was not even 12 years old—during practices to have

300. Paul McLeod, *Filipino Champions Said to Be Overage: Little League: Newspaper in Philippines Says Officials Faked Documents and Lied about Birth Dates at World Series.*, Los Angeles Times (Sep. 4, 1992), https://www.latimes.com/archives/la-xpm-1992-09-04-sp-6363-story.html.
301. The Revised Penal Code, Art. 171.
302. *Ibid.*, Art. 172.
303. Ceej Tantengco, *How Much Does It Cost to Win an Olympic Medal?*, CNN Philippines (Jun. 17, 2019), https://www.cnnphilippines.com/life/culture/2019/6/17/cost-Olympics-Hidilyn-Diaz.html.
304. The Revised Penal Code, Art. 217.
305. *Ibid.*, Art. 222.

intercourse with her.[306] This is textbook statutory rape under the RPC. Statutory rape is committed by a man who shall have carnal knowledge of a woman under 12 years of age.[307] The law is clear. Any sexual intercourse with a victim below twelve—whether with the presence of force, threat, or intimidation or not—is considered rape. The consent of the victim is immaterial. The penalty for statutory rape is *reclusion perpetua* or twenty-forty years in prison.

171. If the victim is over 12, rape is committed when a man has carnal knowledge of a woman through force, threat, or intimidation, when the victim is deprived of reason or otherwise unconscious, or by means of fraudulent machination or grave abuse of authority.[308] The Supreme Court has been consistent in defining carnal knowledge as long as the offender's penis penetrates the victim's labia majora, however slight.[309] In the case of the volleyball coach, it appears he had repeated sexual encounters with his player, some of which occurred after the victim turned 12. While these encounters do not count as statutory rape, these will still be considered rape by means of grave abuse of authority. These will also be considered sexual abuse under Republic Act No. 7610, which will be discussed in the succeeding sections.

172. If the Larry Nassar case had happened in the Philippines, the offender would face sexual assault charges, which is punished with the same gravity as rape. Sexual assault is committed either when a man inserts his penis into another person's mouth or anal orifice or when any person inserts an instrument or object into the genital or anal orifice of another, under the same conditions as rape.[310] The instrument contemplated under the law covers a part of the human body, such as a finger or a tongue. Larry Nassar's sickening and rampant digital penetration of his victims fall squarely within the definition of sexual assault.

173. At a lower tier than rape is the crime of acts of lasciviousness. This crime is committed under the same conditions of rape,[311] but no penetration has occurred, and there was no intent to lie with the victim.[312] The crime envisions acts of lewdness committed against a person of either sex, such as the touching of one's private parts without consent or under duress. Hence, a coach who decides to touch his players inappropriately can face charges of acts of lasciviousness. If the victim is under 18 years of age, the crime is considered child abuse, which carries a heavier penalty.[313]

---

306. Jodee A. Agoncillo, *Family of Minor "Raped" by Volleyball Coach Offers P100-K Reward Money*, The Philippine Daily Inquirer (Jan. 3, 2018), https://newsinfo.inquirer.net/957184/family-of-minor-raped-by-volleyball-coach-offers-p100-k-reward-money.
307. The Revised Penal Code, Art. 266-A(d).
308. *Ibid.*, Art. 266-A(a)-(c).
309. *People v. Campuhan*, 385 Phil. 912 (2000).
310. The Revised Penal Code, Art. 266-A(2).
311. *Ibid.*, Art. 336.
312. *People v. Lizada*, 444 Phil. 67 (2003).
313. *See* Special Protection of Children Against Abuse, Exploitation and Discrimination Act, Re public Act No. 7610 (1992).

174. Under the same title of crimes against chastity as acts of lasciviousness, adultery and concubinage are also criminalized. Adultery is committed by any married woman who has sexual intercourse with a man, not her husband and by the man who has carnal knowledge of the woman knowing her to be married.[314] Concubinage is committed by any husband who keeps a mistress in the conjugal dwelling or has sexual intercourse with a woman, not his wife, under scandalous circumstances.[315] Cohabitation with a woman who is not his wife is also considered concubinage.[316] Note the underlying sexism of the two crimes—a single act of illicit sex by the wife constitutes adultery, while the sex must be under scandalous circumstances for a husband to be charged with concubinage. Sexism aside, it is ironic that it was these acts of adultery and concubinage that had former PBA Commissioner, Emmanuel Eala, being disbarred from the practice of law.[317] While not a criminal case per se, Eala's case is a good indication of how courts deal with adultery and concubinage.

175. Emmanuel Eala served as the PBA Commissioner from 2003 to 2007. However, a few years before his tenure, he began a romantic relationship with Irene Moje—a relationship which would not bode well for Eala in terms of his legal career. Moje was married; in fact, she had just gotten married a few months before their relationship started. Eala was also married with three children. Moje's spurned husband, Joselano Guevarra, found out about the illicit affair after noticing some dubious messages on Moje's phone from Eala. And to make matters worse, Guevara found a love letter penned by Eala addressed to Moje tucked away in their bedroom. The letter spoke of Eala's undying love for Moje, urging her to be "[his] alone … ."[318] The coup de grace in all this was the date of the letter, October 7, 2000, the wedding day of Guevarra and Moje.

176. Understandably upset and embarrassed, Guevarra filed a complaint for disbarment against Eala for "grossly immoral conduct and unmitigated violation of the lawyer's oath."[319] Guevarra cited Eala's adulterous relationship, which he "flaunted" in public. Eala, to his credit, did not deny that he was in an adulterous relationship with Moje. Instead, he maintained that his relationship, adulterous as it was, was not in any way, shape, or form conducted under scandalous circumstances. It was, he claimed, "low profile and known only to the immediate members of their respective families … ."[320]

177. The Supreme Court saw Eala's denial as a negative pregnant (which, as an aside, could not be said of Moje, who in the end was pregnant with Eala's child) and found Eala's actions well within the definition of adultery under the RPC. The Court considered this a clear case of "grossly immoral conduct," a violation of the

314. The Revised Penal Act, Art. 333.
315. *Ibid.*, 334.
316. *Ibid.*
317. *See Guevarra v. Eala*, 555 Phil. 713 (2007).
318. *Ibid.*
319. *Ibid.*
320. *Ibid.*

influence of any adult.[365] The "child" here talks about anyone below the age of 18. Note that the age of sexual consent is 12, but as long as an adult coerces or influences someone below 18 to engage in sex, then that adult will be liable for sexual abuse of a child. An adult may not be held liable for rape, as the coercion might not reach the level necessary to uphold a charge of rape, but he or she can still be held liable for the sexual abuse of a child. Consent is immaterial in sexual abuse cases.[366]

193. The Cybercrime Prevention Act increases the penalty of sexual abuse *if* it was committed by, through, and with the use of information and communications technologies (ICTs).[367] The volleyball coach who would sneak out of practices with his underage player to have intercourse was actually charged with sexual abuse in relation to the Cybercrime Prevention Act.[368] Hence, if he is found to have used ICTs, such as computers or mobile phones, to influence the minor, then his penalty will be increased.

IV. Anti-trafficking in Persons Act

194. Human trafficking has always been a concern whenever big sporting events are held.[369] The mass cross-border movement of people gives human traffickers and opportunity to smuggle people in and out of jurisdictions. Even without the presence of these sporting events in the Philippines, human trafficking is still an alarming issue that the Philippine government has worked hard to prevent, especially with a considerable amount of the Philippine population seeking brighter futures abroad as migrant workers.

195. One way in which the Philippines seeks to address the issue is through the Anti-Trafficking in Persons Act of 2003, which was recently amended in 2012. Sports teams, particularly those involving minors, must be well versed with the provisions of the law, lest the managers and coaches unwittingly engage in human trafficking. Under the rules of the DSWD, Filipino children below 18 years old traveling abroad with someone other than his or her parents must secure a DSWD travel clearance before leaving the country.[370] Without a DSWD clearance, the person accompanying the child may be charged with attempted trafficking in persons,

365. *Olivarez v. Court of Appeals*, 465 SCRA 465, 475 (2005).
366. *Malto v. People*, 533 SCRA 643, 661 (2007).
367. Cybercrime Prevention Act of 2012, Republic Act No. 10175, §6 (2012).
368. *Ibid.*
369. *See* ACAMS Today, *Human Trafficking and Major Sporting Events: The Dark Side of the Super Bowl* (Mar. 28, 2019), https://www.acamstoday.org/human-trafficking-and-major-sporting-events-the-dark-side-of-the-super-bowl/.
370. *See* Department of Social Welfare and Development (DSWD) *Frequently Asked Questions on Clearance for Minors Abroad,* https://www.dswd.gov.ph/frequently-ask-questions-faqs/(last visited Jan. 22, 2020).

a crime committed when a child is transported alone to a foreign country without a valid reason and without the DSWD travel clearance.[371] It is punishable by up to fifteen years in jail.[372]

196. The DSWD clearance is not hard to secure. One needs only to fill out the application form, which can be downloaded from the DSWD website, and submit it to the DSWD Field Office with documents, such as a photocopy of the child's birth certificate and the written consent of both parents (or the solo parent or guardian, as the case may be).[373] The travel clearance is valid for a year from the date of issuance.[374] Note that the DSWD travel clearance is not required for non-Filipino minors.[375] It is also not required when a parent accompanies the minor player on the trip.[376]

V. Hazing

197. Hazing has also been a scourge for educational institutions in the Philippines, with senseless deaths sadly becoming a normal occurrence in universities and law schools. The death of a law student in the country's oldest university—the University of Santo Tomas—prompted an amendment to a two-decade-old law which had already criminalized hazing. The Anti-Hazing Act of 2018 prohibited all forms of hazing and expanded the coverage to all organizations in schools,[377] not merely to fraternities and sororities. As an organization refers to an organized body of people,[378] the prohibition on hazing arguably extends to school-based varsity teams. Previously, hazing in sports teams was arguably not covered by the old hazing law. But with the new amendments in the Anti-Hazing Act of 2018, it now applies to sports teams.

198. Hazing is any act that results in physical or psychological suffering, harm, or injury, inflicted on a recruit, neophyte, applicant, or member as either a prerequisite for admission *or* a requirement for continuing membership in an organization.[379]

199. Hazing is not limited to the meaning normally associated with it—physical violence inflicted by fraternities on their neophytes, like paddling, beating, and whipping. It also includes acts that result in the psychological suffering or harm of a member. Hence, forcing rookies to engage in sexual acts (such as what was done

371. Anti-Trafficking in Persons Act of 2003, Republic Act No. 9208, *amended by* Republic Act No. 10364, §10 (2012).
372. *Ibid.,* §10(b).
373. DSWD, *supra* note 370.
374. *Ibid.*
375. *Ibid.*
376. *Ibid.*
377. Anti-Hazing Act of 2018, Republic Act No. 8049, *amended* by Republic Act No. 11053, §3 (2018).
378. *Ibid.,* §2(c).
379. *Ibid.,* §2(a).

to David Beckham when he was a youngster in Manchester United)[380] or joining team trips to strip clubs and prostitution joints are considered hazing if these result in their psychological harm.

200. Hazing also includes forcing members to drink liquor and alcohol and to consume drugs or other substances.[381] So, forcing rookies to go binge drinking, a common initiation rite among collegiate teams in the Philippines, is hazing. So is forcing a newbie to smoke some pot, which violates not only the Anti-Hazing Act but also the Dangerous Drugs Act of the Philippines.

201. Hazing also includes any activity that tends to humiliate or embarrass, degrade, or endanger wherein a recruit, neophyte, applicant, or member is required to do menial, silly, or foolish tasks.[382] Requiring rookies to strip or undress, another staple in Philippine initiation rites, is illegal hazing, as these activities tend to humiliate or embarrass.

202. A common defense of seniors who engage in hazing is the consent of the rookies. However, the new law explicitly states that prior approval or consent of the rookies to be hazed is immaterial.[383] It is not a defense to any criminal liability that may be imposed on persons who actually planned or participated in the hazing.[384]

203. Not all initiation rites, however, are considered hazing. Hazing does not include customary athletic events or other similar contests or competitions, or any other activity or conduct that furthers a legal and legitimate objective, subject to the prior submission of a medical clearance or certificate.[385] Therefore, tryouts like requiring prospective members to run a certain number of kilometers around the campus are not hazing because these further a legitimate objective. However, the team must require prospective members to submit a medical clearance or certificate before tryouts.

204. Teams may still conduct initiation rites, as long as these do not constitute hazing.[386] However, the law requires teams to submit a written application to the school authorities not later than seven days before the scheduled initiation date.[387]

380. Jack Thorne, *When Do Sport Teams' Initiation Ceremonies Cross Legal Boundaries? Part 1,* Law in Sport (Jul. 17, 2014), https://www.lawinsport.com/more/blogs/squire-patton-boggs/item/when-do-sport-teams-initiation-ceremonies-cross-legal-boundaries-part-1.
381. Anti-Hazing Act of 2018, §2(a).
382. *Ibid.*
383. *Ibid.*, §12.
384. *Ibid.*
385. *Ibid.*, §3.
386. *Ibid.*, §4.
387. *Ibid.*, §4(a).

In any case, these initiation rites must not last for more than three days,[388] and at least two school representatives must be present during the initiation rites to ensure that no hazing is conducted.[389]

205. The penalties for hazing are stiff. If hazing results in death, rape, sodomy or mutilation, those who actually planned or participated in the hazing face twenty to forty years in prison and a fine of PDP 3,000,000.[390] In other cases, the same jail times result in a lesser fine of PDP 2,000,000. The same penalty applies to the advisers of the organizations that conducted the hazing.[391] As a response to the usual stonewalling by fraternity members during investigations of hazing incidents, the law now penalizes anyone who hampers or obstructs any investigation in relation to hazing with a penalty of imprisonment with a duration of twelve years and one day to twenty years and a fine of PDP 1,000,000. These will also apply to members of sports teams who invoke *omerta* in hazing incidents.

VI. Anti-voyeurism Act

206. Sometime around 2007, a football referee was caught taking videos of volleyball players inside the locker rooms in the Blue Eagle Gym at the Ateneo de Manila University. Thankfully, university personnel caught the peeping tom and brought him to justice—or whatever they thought was justice, as reports are mum on what happened to the football referee. If the incident had occurred in 2009, the referee would have been charged with violating the Anti-Photo and Video Voyeurism Act of 2009.[392]

207. The Anti-Photo and Video Voyeurism Act of 2009 was passed after a slew of sex videos emerged online featuring a popular doctor and his bevy of sexual partners, some of which were equally popular actresses and celebrities. These videos were taken without the consent of the actresses, prompting outrage and the quick passage of the law. As the law stands, it is illegal to take a photo or video of the private areas of a person without his or her consent when he or she has a reasonable expectation of privacy.[393] Reasonable expectation of privacy covers instances when the victim believes that he or she can disrobe in privacy without being concerned that his or her private areas will be exposed to the public and caught in video or when the victim believes that his or her private areas will not be visible to the public, regardless of whether that person is in a public or private place.[394]

388. *Ibid.*, §4(d).
389. *Ibid.*, §5.
390. *Ibid.*, §14(a).
391. *Ibid.*, §14(b)(3).
392. *See* Anti-Photo and Video Voyeurism Act of 2009, Republic Act No. 9995 (2009).
393. *Ibid.*, §4(a).
394. *Ibid.*, §3(f).

208. Even as the birth of the law was the sex scandal that rocked the Philippines and derailed the careers of the unwitting stars, the law will apply in the sports setting as well. The peeping tom referee is a prime example of its application. It will also apply to the creepy men who zoom in on the private areas of female volleyball athletes and upload it online, as the law extends to photos or videos that show any portion of a woman's breast or underwear without their consent.[395]

VII. Presidential Decree No. 483

209. As far as sports-specific criminal legislation goes, Presidential Decree (P.D.) No. 483 is as specific as it gets. While passed in 1974 under the unsettling New Society of the dictator President Marcos,[396] the intent of P.D. 483 remains honorable: the promotion of moral and cultural values and the protection of youth from fraudulent schemes that have snaked their way into the once pristine venue of sports. The law seeks to protect the integrity of sports by criminalizing game-fixing, point-shaving, and game machination.

210. Game-fixing is defined as "any arrangement, combination, scheme or agreement by which the result of any game, races or sports contests shall be predicted and/or known other than the basis of the honest playing skill or ability of the players or participants."[397] The law recognizes that sports and games should be won or lost because of the skill or ability of the players—if anyone manipulates the game such that the result is predetermined, then that is game-fixing. There have been murmurings on game-fixing in recent years.

211. Point-shaving is defined as "any such arrangement, combination, scheme or agreement by which the skill or ability of any player or participant in a game, races or sports contests to make points or scores shall be limited deliberately in order to influence the result thereof in favor of one or other team, player or participant therein."[398] Point-shaving is said to be the reason why Far Eastern University basketball standout, Mark Barroca, was dropped from his collegiate team in 2009.[399] His teammate, Mac Baracael, was even shot because of point-shaving allegations a year prior.[400] Both were, however, never charged under P.D. 483.

212. Game machination covers "any other fraudulent, deceitful, unfair or dishonest means, method, manner or practice employed for the purpose of influencing

395. *Ibid.*, §4(a).
396. Penalizing Betting, *Game-Fixing or Point Shaving and Machinations in Sports Contests*, Presidential Decree No. 483, Whereas clause (1974).
397. *Ibid.*, §1(b).
398. *Ibid.*, §1(c).
399. Joey Villar, *Barroca Dropped from FEU for Good,* Philippine Star (Sep. 20, 2009), https://www.philstar.com/sports/2009/09/20/506641/barroca-dropped-feu-good.
400. *Ibid.*

the result of any game, races or sport contest."[401] While doping per se is not criminalized, it is not a far stretch to consider doping as a form of game machination as this involves the use of dishonest means to influence the result of any game or sports contest.

213. As the law was passed nearly fifty years ago, the penalties are still pegged in 1970s valuation. Anyone found guilty under P.D. 483 faces jail time of up to six years and a fine of a paltry PDP 2,000.[402] Congress has sought to amend P.D. 483 and impose stricter penalties. Under House Bill 8204, an athlete faces six to twelve years in prison or a fine of up to PDP 5,000,000 (or both) if convicted of game-fixing. If the athlete is involved in professional sports, he or she will be perpetually disqualified to participate in *any* sports in the country. If the athlete is engaged in amateur sports, then he or she faces perpetual disqualification if found guilty for the second time. In any case, H.B. 8204 has yet to be passed into law.

214. P.D. 483 resurfaced into the public consciousness in mid-2019 as reports of game-fixing hit the Centro Escolar University (CEU) college basketball team. According to news articles, the CEU Scorpions saw seven players removed from its lineup just a day before its PBA D-League quarterfinals against Go-for-Gold-CSB.[403] While the school may impose the appropriate sanctions as an exercise of its academic freedom, the state may also choose to prosecute the players under P.D. 483. The CEU student-athletes, if found guilty, may still play basketball sometime in the future as P.D. 483 does not include perpetual disqualification as a punishment. And in November 2019, then Senator Manny Pacquiao announced that the Maharlika Pilipinas Basketball League—a nationwide basketball league the renaissance man had founded in his free time—suspended the Soccsksargen Marlins for alleged game-fixing as well and referred the matter to the National Bureau of Investigation.[404]

§6. Tax

215. Taxation, as the oft-quoted phrase usually goes, is the lifeblood of the government.[405] Despite the phrase being repeated so many times to the point that it has become a punchline of sorts in legal education, the underlying principle behind it remains as sound as ever. The Philippine government will cease to exist without this inherent power of the state to tax its subjects. The power to tax is inimitable, with

401. Presidential Decree No. 483, §1(d).
402. *Ibid.*, §3(a).
403. Carlo Pamintuan, *Amid Game-Fixing Scandal, Seven-Man CEU Triumphs in PBA D-League QFs,* TV5 ESPN (May 30, 2019), https://tv5.espn.com/basketball/story/_/id/26853624/amid-game-fixing-scandal-seven-man-ceu-triumphs.
404. Reuben Terrado, *MPBL Suspends Soccsksargen Marlins for Alleged Game-Fixing,* Spin.ph Sports (Nov. 4, 2019), https://www.spin.ph/basketball/mpbl-soccsksargen-marlins-suspended-alleged-game-fixing-a795-20191104.
405. *Commissioner of Internal Revenue v. Pineda,* 21 SCRA 105, 110 (1967).

the state generally given wide discretion to tax whomever it chooses.[406] And as the state has the power to determine the subjects of taxation, it is also free to select those lucky few who will be exempt from taxation.[407] Those involved in sports will do well to be conversant in Philippine tax law, as they straddle both sides of the equation, with some entities and individuals subject to tax and some exempt from tax.

216. Philippine taxes can generally be divided into two broad categories: national taxes and local taxes. National taxes are governed by the National Internal Revenue Code (NIRC)[408] and are implemented by the Bureau of Internal Revenue (BIR) of the Department of Finance. National taxes come in different forms—income tax, estate tax, donor's tax, value-added tax (VAT), percentage tax, excise tax, and documentary stamp tax—which may, one way or another, affect a sports stakeholder. Local taxes are governed by the Local Government Code (LGC),[409] which is implemented through delegated legislation in the form of ordinances by LGUs like the province, city, or municipality. These local taxes vary depending on the LGU, and the revenues generated from such accrue exclusively to the LGU involved.[410]

217. Taxpayers normally decry the overlapping system of taxation, as the multiple financial and pecuniary burdens take the guise of double taxation. The Supreme Court, however, has clarified that multiple tax burdens on a single taxpayer do not necessarily trigger the species of double taxation that the Philippine Constitution prohibits. In order for the burdens to take the form of prohibited double taxation, it must constitute direct double taxation which means that the same property or subject matter is taxed twice, for the same purpose, by the same taxing authority, within the same jurisdiction, during the same tax period, with the two taxes of the same nature or character.[411] Hence, a sports team that is taxed by the national government for income tax and by the local government for business taxes cannot raise the defense of double taxation as the taxing authorities are different.

I. Income Tax

218. Under the general principles of income taxation in the Philippines, only resident citizens and domestic corporations are taxable for income sourced worldwide.[412] This is the principle that got Manny Pacquiao into a bit of trouble with the BIR, where the latter alleged the champion boxer—a resident citizen who is liable

406. *Lutz v. Araneta,* 98 Phil. 148, 153 (1955).
407. *Gomez v. Palomar*, 25 SCRA 827, 834 (1968).
408. *See* National Internal Revenue Code, *as amended.*
409. *See* Local Government Code of 1991, Republic Act No. 7160 (1991).
410. *Ibid.,* §129.
411. *Villanueva v. City of Iloilo,* 26 SCRA 578, 594 (1968).
412. National Internal Revenue Code, §23.

for income earned worldwide—failed to include his earnings from his boxing matches in the United States, which lead to a substantial underdeclaration of his income.[413]

219. The other taxpayers—non-resident citizens, overseas contract workers, resident aliens, non-resident aliens, and foreign corporations—are only subject to income tax liability if the respective income is sourced within the Philippines.[414] This leads to the issue of determining the situs of the income, as this will then determine whether an individual, such as a non-resident alien, will be subject to the taxing jurisdiction of the Philippines. This is particularly relevant to foreign athletes, as the situs rules will determine if the BIR can latch on to some of their income if sourced within the Philippine shores.

220. Of particular interest for foreign athletes and sports companies is the situs rules for the performance of service and royalties from the use of intellectual property. Under the NIRC, as long as the service is performed within the Philippines, it will be classified as income within the Philippines, and therefore, subject to Philippine tax laws.[415] An obvious application for this is the talent fees paid to foreign athletes who visit the Philippines to meet fans and hold one-day training camps. For royalties, the rule is that the use of intellectual property—whether copyright, patent, design, trademark, trade brand, or the like—is used in the Philippines, then it will be classified as sourced within the Philippines and subject to Philippine tax laws.[416] Hence, foreign sports brands like Nike or Adidas that enter into licensing agreements with their local counterparts or subsidiaries in the Philippines will be liable for income tax on the royalties they receive from the Philippines for the use of their intellectual property, subject to relief or preferential tax rates under tax treaties.

221. As far as individuals go, the NIRC divides them into resident citizens, non-resident citizens, resident aliens, non-resident aliens engaged in trade or business within the Philippines, and non-resident aliens not engaged in trade or business within the Philippines. The tax rates and liabilities for each type of individual taxpayer differ, and a more nuanced discussion of each is better tackled in a tax-specific article. However, with that said, it is important to note that a recent amendment to the NIRC has largely impacted how athletes now approach their tax liabilities.

222. In late 2017, the Tax Reform for Acceleration and Inclusion Act (TRAIN) was passed, amidst a lot of controversy as to its possible effects on the economy and rising inflation. In any case, TRAIN lumbered along, changing the tax treatment of resident citizens, non-resident citizens, resident aliens, and non-resident aliens engaged in trade or business in the Philippines. This, in turn, affected the tax liabilities of Filipino and foreign athletes and coaches alike.

---

413. *Spouses Pacquiao v. Court of Tax Appeals First Division*, 789 SCRA 19, 23–24 (2016).
414. National Internal Revenue Code, §23.
415. *Ibid.*, §42.
416. *Ibid.*

223. TRAIN groups individuals into three categories for income tax purposes: those who earn purely compensation income; self-employed individuals earning income purely from self-employment or practice of a profession; and mixed-income earners, or those who earn both compensation income and from self-employment or practice of a profession.[417]

224. The first group consists of individuals whose source of income is purely derived from an employer-employee relationship.[418] An example of a purely compensation earner is an athlete who is employed by his team, is paid a salary by the team, and does not earn from other sources, such as endorsements. Players who are recognized employees of their team fall into this category, as long as their salary from their teams is their only source of income. The annual compensation of these individuals will be subject to a graduated table of tax rates, with individuals whose annual compensation does not breach the PDP 250,000 mark exempt from income taxes.[419] As an employee, the athlete's taxes will be withheld by his or her team at a certain rate every payday. These athletes are not required to file their own annual income tax returns as they qualify for substituted filing, which will be the responsibility of their employer.[420]

225. If the athlete is not employed by a team, then he or she falls into the second group—the self-employed individuals earning income purely from self-employment or the practice of a profession. This second group includes professionals like entertainers and athletes who receive promotional and talent fees. Hence, an athlete who earns solely from appearance fees or endorsements will fall under this group. Oddly, professional basketball players in the PBA fall into this group, despite their respective contracts stating they are employees of their teams. This leads to a bifurcated and inconsistent treatment of these PBA players: they are employees for purposes of labor law but independent contractors and professionals for purposes of tax law. An athlete who earns from playing an individual sport will fall under this group as well, as he or she will generally not have a team employer. The same can be said of a student-athlete who earns income from commercials and Instagram posts.

226. The tax liability of the athletes in this second group will depend on his or her gross sales or receipts during the year. If his or her gross sales or receipts exceed PDP 3,000,000, then he or she will be liable under the graduated table of the first group.[421] However, if his or her gross sales or receipts do not exceed PDP 3,000,000, then the athlete is given two choices: use the graduated tax table or pay a flat rate of 8% of the gross sales or receipts in excess of PDP 250,000.[422] If the

417. National Internal Revenue Code, §24.
418. Implementing the Income Tax Provisions of Republic Act No. 10963, Otherwise Known as the "Tax Reform for Acceleration and Inclusion (TRAIN)" Act, Revenue Regulation No. 8-2018, §3(B).
419. National Internal Revenue Code, §24(A)(2)(a).
420. *Ibid.*, §51-A.
421. *Ibid.*, §24(A)(2)(a).
422. *Ibid.*, §24(A)(2)(b).

athlete chooses the 8%, then the athlete will no longer have to pay a percentage tax.[423] In this case, though, the athlete has to signify his or her intention to use the 8% rate in his or her first Quarter Percentage and/or Income Tax Return.

227. The third group is composed of mixed-income earners or those who earn from both compensation and self-employment. In this group falls the professional basketball or football player-employee who also receives professional and talent fees from endorsements. The tax liability of these mixed-income earners is a combination of the first and second groups.

228. First, their team salaries will be taxed under the graduated tax table, which will be withheld by their respective teams. Second, the tax treatment of their income from professional fees will depend on the PDP 3,000,000 threshold, just like the second group. If his or her gross receipts or sales exceed PDP 3,000,000, then these professional fees will also be subject to the tax table.[424] If it does not exceed PDP 3,000,000, then the athlete has the choice of using the tax table or choosing the 8% tax rate.[425] Note, however, that the 8% tax rate for the third group applies to the entire gross receipts or sales and not to whatever excess of PDP 250,000 is left.[426] The BIR has clarified that the reason behind this distinction is that the PDP 250,000 reduction has already been applied in computing the taxes for the mixed-income earner's compensation.[427]

229. TRAIN did not amend the tax treatment of non-resident aliens not engaged in trade or business. This should interest the foreign athletes who visit the Philippines and earn within the jurisdiction as part of promotional tours. A number of National Basketball Association (NBA) stars, such as LeBron James, Steph Curry, the late Kobe Bryant, Damian Lillard, and James Harden, have made their way to the Philippines to boost their brand and image. These NBA stars are considered non-resident aliens not engaged in trade or business because they only have casual transactions in the Philippines, and their visits do not exceed the 180-day limit under the NIRC.[428] As such, they are taxed at 25% of their *entire* income received from all sources within the Philippines.[429]

230. As a final note on athletes, the NIRC states that all prizes and awards granted by athletes both in local and international competitions are exempt from tax. However, these competitions must be sanctioned by the relevant NSA. And, as an additional requirement, the NSA must be accredited by the POC. In 2000, the BIR opined that the cash prize won by Chess Grandmaster, Joey Antonio, Jr., was not

423. *Ibid.*
424. National Internal Revenue Code, §24(A)(2)(c)(2)(b).
425. *Ibid.,* §24(A)(2)(c)(2)(a).
426. Bureau of Internal Revenue, Revenue Memorandum Circular No. 5-2018 (Jan. 16, 2018).
427. *Ibid.*
428. National Internal Revenue Code, §25(A).
429. *Ibid.,* §25(B).

exempt from income tax because the competition was organized by a sports association not recognized by the POC.[430] In 2005, Antonio sought reconsideration but to no avail.[431]

231. Corporations are taxed in a more straightforward manner. Domestic corporations are taxed depending on their net taxable income and total assets: those whose net taxable income does not exceed PDP 5,000,000 and total assets do not exceed PDP 100,000,000 are taxed 20% of their taxable income, while those over the said thresholds are taxed 25% of their taxable income—with beginning their fourth year of operations both possibly subject to the minimum corporate income tax (MCIT) rate of 2% of their gross income if their tax liability under the 20/25% rate is less than the MCIT for the taxable year.[432] Domestic corporations include business partnerships, no matter how these are created.[433] Hence, for-profit companies in the sports business must pay either the 20/25% regular corporate income tax rate, depending on their income and assets, or the MCIT.

232. As a bulk of sports occur within the educational sphere, the taxation of schools is important to consider. Schools fall within two broad categories: non-stock, non-profit educational institutions and proprietary educational institutions.

233. Non-stock, non-profit educational institutions are given special tax-exempt status by the Constitution itself. Under the Constitution, all revenues and assets of these non-stock, non-profit educational institutions are exempt from taxes as long as these are used actually, directly, and exclusively for educational purposes.[434] This tax exemption is broad, as it covers all taxes, such as income tax and real property tax (RPT), that would have been imposed by LGUs if not for the constitutional exemption. Hence, a school that has an athletic facility that it earns income from and which it uses for the athletic pursuits of its students is exempt from both income tax on its profits and the RPT on the facility, as long as the school can prove that both the profits and the facility are actually, directly, and exclusively for educational purposes.[435]

234. While not exempt, proprietary educational institutions are still given special preference under the NIRC. Proprietary educational institutions are taxed at a special rate of 10% of taxable income. This, however, hikes up to the regular corporate income tax rate if the school's gross income from unrelated activities exceeds 50% of the total gross income of the institution.[436] To qualify for this special rate,

430. BIR Ruling No. 026-00 (Jun. 13, 2000).
431. BIR Ruling No. DA-038-05 (2005).
432. National Internal Revenue Code, §27, as amended by Republic Act No. 11534, Otherwise Known as the "Corporate Recovery and Tax Incentives for Enterprises (CREATE) Law." Note: The MCIT from July 1, 2020 to June 30, 2023 is 1% of gross income.
433. *Ibid.*, §22 (B).
434. Phil. Const. Art. XIV, §4(3).
435. *Commissioner of Internal Revenue v. De La Salle University, Inc.*, 808 SCRA 156, 175 (2016).
436. National Internal Revenue Code, §27(B). Note: The special rate is 1% of taxable income from July 1, 2020 to June 30, 2023.

the educational institution must be a private school with a permit to operate by the Department of Education (DepEd), the Commission on Higher Education (CHED), or the Technical Education and Skills Development Authority.[437] Additionally, the BIR has opined that the educational institution must be non-profit as well.[438]

235. PAGCOR, ever the subject of controversy because of its mandate to regulate gambling in the Philippines, has also had its fair share of taxation issues. Prior laws exempted PAGCOR from the payment of income tax. However, with the passage of R.A. 9337 in 2005, PAGCOR's tax-exempt status was removed.[439] This led to the issue of whether PAGCOR was subject to the regular corporate income tax rate or the franchise tax stated in its charter. In 2014, the Supreme Court resolved the matter stating that PAGCOR's income from its gaming operations was subject to its 5% franchise tax under its charter, but its income from unrelated activities would be subject to the regular income tax rate.[440] The confusion then spread to the tax liability of PAGCOR's contractees and licensees, and this was finally resolved in 2016 when the Supreme Court stated that PAGCOR's contractees and licensees were subject to the same rule.[441]

236. NSAs are exempt from income tax because non-stock corporations or associations organized and operated exclusively for athletic purposes are considered tax-exempt corporations.[442] However, no part of its income or assets should belong or inure to the benefit of any member, organizer, officer, or any specific person.[443] The no-inurement rule is strictly construed by the BIR, and numerous rulings have stated that the mere receipt by trustees of per diems during meetings is enough to remove the tax-exempt status of the association.[444] Note that these must be both organized and operated for athletic purposes. This means that its incorporation documents must all point to the laudable goal of athletics and that its actual regular activities must be done exclusively for athletic purposes.[445] Further, the tax-exempt status does not extend to profits it earns from for-profit activities or those it receives from any of its properties, real or personal.[446] Finally, donations and contributions to domestic corporations or associations organized and operated exclusively for sports

---

437. *Ibid.*
438. Clarifying the Inurement Prohibition under s. 30 of the National Internal Revenue Code of 1997, Revenue Memorandum Circular No. 51-2014 (BIR, Jun. 6, 2014).
439. *Philippine Amusement and Gaming Corporation (PAGCOR) v. Bureau of Internal Revenue*, 645 SCRA 338, 355 (2011).
440. *Ibid.*, 744 SCRA 712, 729 (2014).
441. *Bloomberry Resorts and Hotels, Inc. v. Bureau of Internal Revenue,* 800 SCRA 123, 139–140 (2016).
442. National Internal Revenue Code, §30 (E).
443. *Ibid.*
444. BIR Ruling 560-17.
445. Circularizes the pertinent portions of the Supreme Court Decision in G.R. Nos. 195909 and 195960 entitled "*Commissioner of Internal Revenue v. St. Luke's Medical Center, Inc.*," on the income tax treatment of proprietary non-profit hospitals and on the 1998 deficiency income tax liability of St. Luke's Medical Center, Inc. on the revenues it derived from services to paying patients and their tax implications and implementation thereof, Revenue Memorandum Circular No. 67-2012 (BIR, Oct. 31, 2012).
446. National Internal Revenue Code, §30.

development whose income does not inure to the benefit of private individuals are allowed as either partial or full deductions for a taxpayer's gross income, depending on if the organization has been accredited as a non-government organization.[447]

II. Value-Added Tax

237. VAT is imposed on "any person who, in the course of trade or business, sells, barters, exchanges, leases goods or properties, renders services" in the Philippines and on "any person who imports goods" into the Philippines.[448]

238. The list of sales and services subject to VAT in the law is not exclusive, as the current interpretation of VAT is that it applies to all services and sales as long as it is performed in the course of trade or business. Hence, athletes who have endorsements are liable for VAT on their talent fees, as these are services performed in the course of their trade or business. The same can be said for the sale or lease of intellectual property. Generally, the rate imposed on these transactions is 12%.[449]

239. The TRAIN Act, however, has increased the VAT registration threshold to those persons whose annual gross receipts or sales exceed PDP 3,000,000.[450] Hence, those athletes whose annual gross sales or receipts do not reach the threshold are exempt from the payment of the 12% VAT. Another group of athletes who are not liable for VAT are those employed by their respective teams (such as PBA players), as services rendered by individuals pursuant to an employer-employee relationship are explicitly excluded from VAT.[451]

III. Tax Evasion and Remedies

240. Athletes have often caught the eye of the BIR in issues relating to the payment—or the lack thereof—of proper taxes. Two high-profile athletes come to mind when it comes to dealing with tax issues and the BIR: basketball behemoth, Asi Taulava, and senator-boxer, Manny Pacquiao. Both cases are discussed below.

241. Asi Taulava is a Filipino-Tongan basketball player who, as of this writing, still plays in the PBA at the age of 41. Taulava is one of the most popular professional basketball players and was the PBA Most Valuable Player in 2003. However, he was charged with willfully failing to pay deficiency income taxes and VAT for

447. *Ibid.*, §34(H).
448. *Ibid.*, §105.
449. *Ibid.*, §§106 and 108. Export sales and services are given a 0% rate, depending on certain requirements and conditions.
450. *Ibid.*, §236(G)(1).
451. *Ibid.*, §109(I).

the taxable year 2004. Willful failure to pay taxes is a criminal offense under section 255 of the NIRC. In common parlance, it is known as tax evasion. The tax evasion case against Taulava concluded on November 3, 2017, when the Court of Tax Appeals (CTA) First Division ruled for the big man and acquitted him of tax evasion.[452]

242. In ruling for the Fil-Tongan, the Court laid down the elements for conviction under section 255. To convict Taulava, the BIR had to prove the elements of the crime: first, the accused was required by law to pay any tax at the time or times required by law; second, the accused failed to pay the required tax; and third, the accused willfully failed to pay such tax.[453] The CTA stated that the second and third elements all depend on the existence of the first because the failure to pay the tax is conditioned on one's tax liability.[454]

243. The issue then revolved around the issue of whether Taulava was required by law to pay any tax at the time required by law. The CTA noted that the requirement to pay any Philippine tax arises in two ways. The first is through a taxpayer's voluntary self-assessment—which is the method employed by most Filipinos who report and pay their own taxes.[455] The second is through an assessment issued by the Commissioner of Internal Revenue (CIR) or his or her representative. This government-issued assessment is a demand to pay tax or deficiency taxes to the BIR.[456]

244. Taulava's case focused on the second way, as the center was supposedly required to pay taxes based on a tax assessment issued by the BIR. However, the BIR failed to prove that Taulava was assessed in the first place.[457] As such, he was not legally required to pay deficiency taxes. In turn, he could not have willfully failed to pay the tax, as he was not required to pay to begin with.[458]

245. In its defense, the BIR argued that it had sent Taulava the Formal Letter of Demand and Final Assessment Notices (FLD-FAN) via registered mail.[459] In response, Taulava denied he ever received the FLD-FAN.[460] The BIR argued that it was presumed that the FLD-FAN was received by Taulava, as it was sent by registered mail. This disputable presumption applies when the BIR is able to prove that the FLD-FAN was *actually* mailed.[461] However, the BIR failed in this regard, as they failed to present the registry receipt issued by the Bureau of Posts, the Registry Return Card, or even certification from the Bureau of Posts. With the presumption

452. *People v. Taulava,* C.T.A. Crim Case No. O-309 (2017).
453. *Ibid.,* p. 31.
454. *Ibid.,* p. 32.
455. *Ibid.*
456. *Ibid.,* p. 33.
457. *Ibid.*
458. *Ibid.*
459. *Ibid.,* p. 34.
460. *Ibid.*
461. *Ibid.*

inapplicable to the BIR and Taulava's explicit denial, the CTA found that Taulava never received the FLD-FAN and, therefore, was never assessed.[462] He was acquitted.[463]

246. Senator Manny Pacquiao's tax woes with the BIR have been widely publicized in the Philippines. It has been a running joke that regardless of the result of Pacquiao's boxing matches, the winner, in the end, is the BIR. Pacquiao, however, got one over the BIR in a Supreme Court case decided in 2016.[464] In *Spouses Pacquiao v. the Court of Tax Appeals First Division and the Commissioner of Internal Revenue*, at issue was Pacquiao's alleged deficiency of income taxes and VAT for the taxable years 2008 and 2009.[465] The amount was not small by any stretch of the imagination. In 2008, the BIR alleged that Pacquiao had deficiency income tax in the amount of more than PDP 700 million and VAT of PDP 4 million.[466] For 2009, Pacquiao's deficiency income tax was alleged to have topped the PDP 1 billion mark, with his VAT liability exceeding PDP 24 million.[467] In total, Pacquiao was alleged to have owed the government more than PDP 2 billion.[468]

247. Pacquiao questioned the assessment in the CTA and asked that warrants of distraint and levy on his properties be suspending pending the case.[469] The CTA granted Pacquiao's motion but required him to pay a cash bond of around PDP 3 billion or post a bond of PDP 4 billion.[470] Pacquiao took issue on the requirement of the bond, given its exorbitant amount and because of the means employed by the BIR to come up with the assessment.[471] Pacquiao claimed he was denied due process.[472]

248. The Supreme Court ruled in favor of the boxer.[473] It stated that the CTA could dispense with the requirement of the bond if it is determined that the CIR's method of computing Pacquiao's liability was not sanctioned by law.[474] The case was remanded back to the CTA to determine if Pacquiao's rights were violated and if a bond was indeed needed; all the while, the warrants were suspended without the need for the bond.[475]

---

462. *Ibid.*, p. 39.
463. *Ibid.*, p. 40.
464. *Spouses Pacquiao,* 789 SCRA at 55.
465. *Ibid.*, at 23.
466. *Ibid.*, at 30.
467. *Ibid.*, at 31.
468. *Ibid.*
469. *Ibid.*, at 32.
470. *Ibid.*, at 33–34.
471. *Ibid.*, at 34.
472. *Ibid.*, at 41.
473. *Ibid.*, at 55.
474. *Ibid.*, at 45.
475. *Ibid.*, at 46.

IV. Local Government Taxes

249. Under the Philippine Constitution, LGUs have the power to create their own sources of revenue and to levy taxes and other fees, subject only to the Constitution and limitations set by Congress.[476] This limitation set by Congress can be found in the LGC of 1991, which enumerates the basic rules for local taxation.[477] Any tax ordinance or revenue-raising measure must comply with the LGC. Whatever revenue raised or collected by the LGU accrues exclusively to the collecting LGU.[478]

250. One basic limitation for LGUs is that they are not allowed to levy taxes, charges, or duties on any subject already taxed by the national government under the NIRC. This limitation was put to the test in *Philippine Basketball Association v. Court of Appeals*.[479] The case began when the CIR—the tax collecting representative of the national government—assessed the PBA with deficiency amusement tax.[480] The PBA refused to pay, arguing that it was subject to the local tax on amusement places payable to the local government, not the national government.[481]

251. The Supreme Court ruled against the PBA, stating that it was indeed liable to the national government under a special law.[482] The Court went through the legislative history of local taxes on amusement places and found that the authority to tax professional basketball games has always been excluded from the ambit of the imposition.[483] The local tax on amusement places, the Court said, was imposed on theaters, cinematographers, concert halls, circuses and other places of amusement.[484] Using the principle of *ejusdem generis*, the Court found that the PBA was not technically a place of amusement.[485] Hence, the PBA was liable to the national government, not the LGU.[486]

252. Following the same train of thought, the Supreme Court has likewise ruled that resorts, swimming pools, and tourist spots are not amusement places within the meaning of the law and are, therefore, not subject to local tax.[487] In order to fall within the ambit of local amusement tax, the place must be one where people flock for the staging of spectacles or the holding of public shows or exhibitions.[488]

---

476. Phil. Const. Art. X, §5.
477. Local Government Code, §129.
478. Phil. Const. Art. X, §5.
479. *Philippine Basketball Association v. Court of Appeals,* 337 SCRA 358, 361 (2000).
480. *Ibid.,* at 363.
481. *Ibid.,* at 370.
482. *Ibid.,* 364.
483. *Ibid.,* at 366–368.
484. *Ibid.,* at 366.
485. *Ibid.,* at 365.
486. *Ibid.,* at 370.
487. *Pelizloy Realty Corporation v. Province of Benguet,* 695 SCRA 491, 505 (2013).
488. *Ibid.,* at 507.

253. In the same light, golf courses are not subject to local amusement tax.[489] In 2016, the Supreme Court ruled that people do not go to golf courses to watch the spectacle of other people playing golf.[490] Instead, they go there to, yes, play golf.[491]

254. While golf courses are not subject to local amusement tax, these water-guzzling stretches of grass are subject to RPT, another local government imposition separate from local taxes. Real property may be taxed by provinces, cities, and municipalities within Metro Manila.[492] The basic rule is that real property is subject to RPT unless specifically exempted by the LGC. Unfortunately, golf courses are not among those real properties exempted from RPT.

255. This, of course, does not preclude the possibility that a golf course—or any sports venue—will ever be exempted from RPT. If the sports venue is owned by the government or any of its political subdivisions (and its beneficial use has not been granted to a taxable person) or is owned by a charitable institution and uses actually, exclusively, and directly for charitable purposes, then the venue would be exempt from RPT.[493] Finally, as alluded to earlier, the assets of non-profit, non-stock educational institutions which are actually, directly, and exclusively used for educational purposes are exempt from all kinds of tax.[494] Hence, a school-owned sports facility or stadium will be exempt.

§7. Sports Justice

256. The Philippines currently does not have any set mode of dispute resolution for sports. Even amidst calls for a robust system for sports arbitration (similar to the workings of the Court of Arbitration for Sport), sports disputes result in court cases—adding to the already clogged dockets of Philippine courts.[495] Injunctions and temporary restraining orders are normally sought out by aggrieved athletes who question eligibility rules, such as what happened in 2017 when a college player sued the UAAP over an age restriction.[496] Other jurisdictions would have ushered the dispute to arbitration or mediation, but not in the Philippines. Sadly, if the internal rules of an organization like an NSA or an athletic association fail to resolve issues, these end up in court.

---

489. *Alta Vista Gold and Country Clubs v. City of Cebu*, 781 SCRA 335, 361 (2016).
490. *Ibid.*, at 360–361.
491. *Ibid.*, at 361.
492. Local Government Code, §200.
493. *Ibid.*, §234.
494. Phil. Const. Art. XIV §4(3).
495. Ignatius Michael D. Ingles, *Keeping Sports out of Courts: Philippine Sports Arbitration (Part III)*, Batas Sportiva (Oct. 27, 2016), https://batassportiva.com/2016/10/27/keeping-sports-out-of-courts-philippines-sports-arbitration-part-iii/.
496. Ignatius Michael D. Ingles, *#LetRobPlay: Explaining Rob Ricafort's Eligibility Case v. The UAAP*, Batas Sportiva (Oct. 19, 2017), https://batassportiva.com/2017/10/19/letrobplay-explaining-rob-ricaforts-eligibility-case-vs-the-uaap/.

257. In early 2022, the Philippine Dispute Resolution Center, Inc. (PDRCI), fresh off approving its sports mediation rules and accrediting its first batch of sports mediators, helped the PSC in the mediation proceedings between Olympian EJ Obiena and PATAFA.[497] In May 2022, the PDRCI and GAB signed a memorandum of agreement for sports dispute resolution.[498]

§8. Student-Athletes Protection Act

258. Before the SAPA was passed in 2015, college and university athletic associations had free rein in implementing their own residency and eligibility rules for participation in interschool competitions. This, however, soon became a national issue in 2014 when the UAAP enacted a rule that prohibited high school graduates who moved to a different school for college from immediately playing for their new schools. The rule mandated transferees to sit out two years before they could suit up for their new schools. The UAAP, in its defense, stated that the rule prevented the rampant piracy that was occurring between schools. It was a measure to maintain the veneer of amateurism because it reasoned that if students were allowed to transfer from one school to another, there was little or no difference to the situation of professional athletes who could freely move from one team to another. This was questioned and scrutinized for obvious reasons, particularly by education advocates who reckoned there were a multitude of non-sports-related reasons why a student-athlete may choose to enroll in a different school. Senate hearings were held, and soon the SAPA was born. It remains the only law that imposes any direct restriction on athletic associations.

259. The SAPA begins with the laudable pronouncement that a student-athlete is a student first.[499] It also sets to define who a student-athlete is. The SAPA defines student-athlete as any currently enrolled student who is a member of any of the school's athletic teams or programs and who represents *or* has intentions of representing the school in interschool competitions and is enrolled in at least a minimum full-time curricular program.[500] However, the SAPA leaves it up to the different athletic associations to determine eligibility requirements, such as grade-point averages or other academic requirements. With that said, a student-athlete must also be in good standing to be eligible to represent the school in competitions.[501] What this "good standing" actually means is left unanswered by the law.

260. The SAPA essentially limits the power of athletic associations to craft their own residency rules. To be clear, residency rules usually require transferring student-athletes to sit out a year or two before they can start playing for their new school. Whatever residency requirements associations might come up with *must*

497. PSC Press Statement (Mar. 30, 2022).
498. On file with the Author.
499. Student-Athletes Protection Act, §2.
500. *Ibid.*, §3(c).
501. *Ibid.*

comply with the SAPA. For a student-athlete who just graduated high school and is enrolling in a college or university, no residency requirement shall be imposed.[502] For high school student-athletes who wish to transfer to a different high school, no residency requirement shall be imposed as well.[503] However, if the student transfers to a school within the same athletic association, a one-year residency requirement may be imposed.[504] For college and university student-athletes, the athletic association may impose a one-year residency requirement, regardless if the student-athlete transfers to a school within the same athletic association or not.[505] As can be seen in the rules, the SAPA seeks to work out a compromise between the real issue of student-athlete piracy and the equally pressing issue of allowing student-athletes to study wherever they wish to do so.

261. The residency rules imposed by SAPA for local student-athletes apply to Filipino student-athletes from other countries.[506] Hence, repatriating Filipino student-athletes who previously studied abroad and are looking to play for a local school will be protected from residency rules that seek to impose time limits beyond the allowable provisions of the SAPA. The same cannot be said about foreign student-athletes who wish to study and play for a local school. The SAPA is explicit in giving athletic associations free rein on how to deal with residency requirements for student-athletes who are foreign imports.[507] This has led to an athletic association banning foreign student-athletes altogether.[508]

262. To add some teeth to the law, the SAPA has banned retaliatory acts against student-athletes who wish to transfer to a different school. These prohibited acts include filing administrative charges against the student for violation of school rules, requiring payment of a previously granted tuition scholarship, refusing or delaying the issuance of grades and school clearance documents, giving incomplete grades in subjects which the student-athlete is exempted by virtue of being a student-athlete, and imposing other forms of punishment.[509]

263. Aside from setting residency rules, the SAPA also seeks to protect student-athletes from commercialization. Another goal is to keep student-athletes as students first. It does this by enumerating the kinds of benefits and incentives a school may grant a student-athlete. The list of allowable benefits and incentives includes the usual tuition scholarships, which also include school-related expenses like books

---

502. Student-Athletes Protection Act, §4(a).
503. *Ibid.*, §4(b).
504. *Ibid.*
505. *Ibid.*, §4(c).
506. *Ibid.*, §4(d).
507. *Ibid.*, §4.
508. Beatrice Go, *NCAA to Ban Foreign Players Starting Season 96 in* 2020, Rappler (Jun. 19, 2018), https://www.rappler.com/sports/university/ncaa/205265-ban-foreign-players-imports-2020.
509. Student-Athletes Protection Act, §§4(d)(1)–(5).

and other learning materials,[510] full board and lodging expenses,[511] school and athletic uniforms,[512] reasonable monthly allowances (which are to be determined by the respective athletic associations),[513] medical examinations and consultations, emergency medical services, life and medical insurance,[514] and other reasonable benefits that would further enhance the student-athlete's academic and athletic performance.[515]

264. While the list seems extensive, it is quite porous in its application. It is a well-known secret that schools have remained unaffected by the SAPA's rules on incentives, especially when it comes to enticing prized student-athletes. Whispers abound in the collegiate sports circles of well-endowed schools with even more well-endowed alumni backers offering everything from grocery franchises to job security to a recruit's family to students. And despite a seeming limitation on allowances for student-athletes, these are still determined by the different athletic associations, whose boards are composed of school representatives who have their own school's interests to protect. Likewise, the SAPA only focuses on residency rules and allowable benefits, leaving athletic associations free to craft their own rules on touchy subjects like player tampering, which gained national news in 2019 when a university standout was reportedly being pirated by two other universities midseason and the lack of association rules against it.[516]

265. For violations, the SAPA imposes liability on school officials, athletic directors, coaches and their staff, administrators, alumni, and school representatives.[517] In fact, even the athletic associations or the schools may be held liable if they knowingly permit or fail to prevent SAPA violations.[518] Complaints may be filed by almost anyone as the law allows complaints to come from student-athlete, his/her parents or guardians, member schools or their alumni, or any person or any entity on behalf of a student-athlete who, or a school which, may be affected by any SAPA violation.[519]

266. Violations must first be reported to the athletic association.[520] These athletic associations have the duty to investigate, either on their own or based on a complaint, and impose penalties, such as suspending or banning student-athletes or

---

510. *Ibid.*, §5(a).
511. Student-Athletes Protection Act, §5(b).
512. *Ibid.*, §5(c).
513. *Ibid.*, §5(d).
514. *Ibid.*, §5(e). Insurance should at least be shouldered by the schools. For schools which do not offer insurance to take care of its student-athletes who get injured while wearing your school colors, what is up with that?
515. *Ibid.*, §5(f).
516. Randolph B. Leongson, *"Poaching" Attempts Cited as Reason Behind UST Benching of Rhenz Abando,* Spin.ph (Oct. 17, 2019), https://www.spin.ph/basketball/uaap-men/poaching-attempts-cited-as-reason-behind-ust-benching-of-rhenz-abando-a2437-20191017.
517. Student-Athletes Protection Act, §8(b).
518. *Ibid.*
519. *Ibid.*, §8(a).
520. *Ibid.*, §8(c).

schools from competing. However, recourse can also be made straight to the DepEd or the CHED if the athletic association has yet to act on a complaint or if the athletic association is itself the respondent.[521] If urgent action is required, the SAPA allows relief from courts if there is no other plain, speedy, and adequate remedy in the ordinary course of law.[522]

267. Schools which have been found to have violated the SAPA can be suspended from participating in athletic events and/or be slapped with a fine ranging from PDP 100,000 to PDP 1,000,000.[523] Athletic associations can also be slapped with a fine ranging from PDP 100,000 to PDP 1,000,000.[524]

268. Despite the policy against commercialization, the SAPA's prohibition is directed toward schools. The law prohibits *schools* from commercializing their student-athletes. It does not prohibit student-athletes from monetizing their popularity. Hence, a student-athlete can enter into endorsement contracts if he or she so chooses, which in fact, the most popular student-athletes have done. It also does not prevent athletic associations and schools from entering into contracts that monetize the popularity of amateur sports with third parties, as can be seen in the mindboggling number of commercials and product placement segments during a collegiate basketball or volleyball game.

§9. National Athletes and Coaches Benefits and Incentives Act

269. In 2015, R.A. 10699 or the NACBIA was passed to bolster the benefits and incentives for national athletes and coaches. The NACBIA amended a previous law which had also granted benefits by increasing the monetary amounts and including AWDs in the incentive scheme.

270. Under the NACBIA, national athletes are Filipino citizens who are members of the national training pool and are accredited by both the POC and the PSC.[525] Also included are AWDs who have been recognized by the PSC and the National Paralympic Committee of the Philippines (NPC PHIL) and who have represented the country in international sports competitions.[526] National coaches are Filipino coaches of national athletes and members of the national coaches training pool who have been recognized and accredited by the PSC and the POC (or the PSC and the NPC PHIL if they coach AWDs).[527]

271. The monetary incentives depend on the competition and the medals won by the national athlete. Under the law, the incentives are as provided in Table 2.

521. *Ibid.*
522. Student-Athletes Protection Act, §8(g).
523. *Ibid.*, §8(f)(1).
524. *Ibid.*, §8 (f) (2).
525. National Athletes and Coaches Benefits and Incentives Act, §3(c).
526. *Ibid.*
527. *Ibid.*, §3(d).

Table 2 Monetary Incentives under the SAPA

Competition/Medal Rank	*Gold*	*Silver*	*Bronze*
Olympics	PDP 10,000,000	PDP 5,000,000	PDP 2,000,000
Youth Olympics, and Paralympic Games	PDP 5,000,000	PDP 2,500,000	PDP 1,000,000
Asian Games, Asian Winter Games, Asian Indoor Martial Arts Games	PDP 2,000,000	PDP 1,000,000	PDP 400,000
Asian Para Games, and World-level competitions held at least every two years with at least forty-five countries participating	PDP 1,000,000	PDP 500,000	PDP 200,000
Asian Beach Games, Asian-level competitions held at least every two years with at least twenty-five countries participating, and Qualifying competitions for World-level and Asian-level games	PDP 500,000	PDP 250,000	PDP 100,000
South East Asian (SEA) Games	PDP 300,000	PDP 150,000	PDP 60,000
ASEAN Para Games	PDP 150,000	PDP 75,000	PDP 30,000

In addition, national athletes and other athletes who set Philippine records or surpass ranking in any measurable international sports competition are entitled to cash incentives to be determined by the PSC. After Hidilyn Diaz won the country's first gold medal in Tokyo 2020, issues arose on whether all her monetary incentives—from the government and private sponsors—would be taxable.[528] The BIR thereafter clarified that government incentives are non-taxable, but prizes, donations, and incentives from private backers are taxable.[529]

272. For team events, members divide the cash incentives among themselves. For those less than five in the team, the team gets the same amounts as individual athletes, but the amount must be divided equally among them; For competitions with more than five participants, each member gets 25% of the cash incentives allocated for individual athletes.[530] For those who medal in demonstration and exhibition sports events in the Olympics, national athletes are entitled to 25% of the cash incentives for individual medalists.[531]

528. Ignatius Michael D. Ingles, *Hidilyn's Golden 33M: Taxable or Not?*, Batas Sportiva (Jul. 27, 2021), https://batassportiva.com/2021/07/27/hidilyns-golden-33m-taxable-or-not/.
529. BIR Press Statement (Jul. 29, 2021).
530. *Ibid.*
531. *Ibid.*

273. Sadly, AWDs are only entitled to just half of the incentives. A Filipino who bags gold in the Olympics is entitled to PDP 10,000,000, but a Filipino who bags gold in the Paralympics is only entitled to PDP 5,000,000. A certain legislator had reasoned that AWDs were not entitled to any benefits before the NACBIA was passed, implying that they should at least be thankful for the incentives.[532] This, of course, should not be the case, as it is a distinction based on a person's disability which seems to violate the Constitution's equal protection clause.[533]

274. National coaches are entitled to half of the cash incentives for medalists.[534] In the case of more than one coach, the incentives will be divided among themselves.[535] To qualify, the coach must have personally trained and rendered service to the winning athlete or team at least six months prior to the international competition.[536] The coach must get a certification from the athlete or the team captain, which should also be attested by the appropriate NSA.[537]

275. Aside from these monetary incentives, national athletes and coaches are also entitled to discounts in certain establishments. They must be registered with the PSC and the POC (as either a national athlete or coach) and present a valid National Team ID and booklet provided by the PSC.[538] Discounts and requirements are as provided in Table 3.

Table 3 Discounts and Applicable Requirements under the NACBIA

Domestic Transportation Privileges	– 20% on all fares for domestic air and sea travel. – 20% on all fares for public land transportation.
Hotels and Lodging	– 20% on room accommodations and other amenities offered by the hotel or establishment. – 20% discount applies to hotel-based restaurants, barbershops, parlors, saunas, gyms, and internet facilities.

532. *See* Ignatius Michael D. Ingles, *Equal Protection: Athletes with Disabilities and RA 10699*, Batas Sportiva (Sep. 17, 2016), https://batassportiva.com/2016/09/17/equal-protection-athletes-with-disabilities-and-ra-10699/.
533. *Ibid.*
534. National Athletes and Coaches Benefits and Incentives Act, §9.
535. *Ibid.*
536. *Ibid.*
537. *Ibid.*
538. Rules and Regulations Implementing Republic Act No. 10699, entitled "An Act Expanding the Coverage of Incentives Granted to National Athletes and Coaches, Appropriating Funds Therefor, Repealing for the Purpose Republic Act No. 9064, also known as the 'National Athletes, Coaches and Trainers Benefits and Incentives Act of 2001' or 'Sports Benefits and Incentives Act of 2001'," Revenue Regulations No. 13-2020 (BIR, May 27, 2020).

Restaurants	– 20% on food, drinks, dessert, and other consumable items. – Also applies to take-out/take-home/drive-thru orders as long as the national athlete or coach is present and personally ordering and presenting his or her National Team ID. – Also applies to delivery, as long as the National Team ID number is given when making the order and the ID Card and the booklet are presented upon delivery.
Recreation Centers and Gyms	– 20% on fees, charges, and rentals for any sports facilities, equipment, and other accessories for sports. – This includes renting out a venue for working out or training (like bowling lanes, tennis courts, gyms, ballroom dancing). – Exclusive sports and country clubs are not mandated to grant the 20% discount, but the independent concessionaire-restaurants inside the clubs are required to grant the 20% discount.
Medicine and Drug Purchases	– 20% for the purchase of generic or branded medicines and drugs. – 20% for the purchase of vitamins and supplements prescribed by a doctor. – The booklet must be presented to avail of this discount.
Sports Equipment Purchases	– 20% on the purchase of sports equipment for the actual and exclusive use of the national athlete or coach. – This includes game equipment (like balls, nets, goals, and bats) and player equipment (like footwear and training equipment). – To avail of this discount though, the NSA must endorse the purchase by noting it in the athlete's or coach's Booklet and the Booklet must then be presented.
Admission Fees	– 20% discount for admission fees to movie theaters, concert halls, and other similar places of cultures, leisure, and amusement.

276. The implementation of this discount scheme has been shoddy and haphazard, as establishments simply were not aware of the matter. The Athletes' Commission of the POC has done well to raise awareness of these law-mandated discounts, and some businesses have thankfully been honoring the discounts. In turn, the establishments may claim the discounts as tax deductions to lower their taxable income. After years of waiting, the BIR finally released the revenue regulations for its implementation in May 2020.[539]

539. *Ibid.*

277. National athletes and coaches also get free medical and dental consultations in government hospitals and similar establishments anywhere in the country.[540] They are also prioritized in government livelihood projects and national housing programs.[541] And, of course, they are free to use PSC living quarters and training centers.[542]

278. National athletes who win in regular major international sports competitions are entitled to full-tuition scholarships from state colleges or universities.[543] Those from private colleges and universities have to check with their respective schools, as these private educational institutions are merely encouraged by law to grant scholarships.[544]

279. Finally, the law also grants retirement and death benefits to national athletes and coaches. A retiring national athlete or coach who has coached a winning national athlete is entitled to 25% of his or her total cash incentives during his or her career.[545] And death benefits up to PDP 30,000 are given upon the death of any national and coach to the spouse or children of the deceased. If the athlete or coach does not have a spouse or children, the benefits can be claimed by his or her parents and, in their absence, his or her siblings.[546]

540. National Athletes and Coaches Benefits and Incentives Act, §4(c).
541. *Ibid.*, §4(f) & (g).
542. *Ibid.*, §4(h).
543. *Ibid.*, §5.
544. *Ibid.*
545. *Ibid.*, §6.
546. *Ibid.*

Part II. Sport and Employment

Chapter 1. General Issues

280. Players face a number of issues in terms of employment law, starting with the most basic issue of whether they are considered employees of their teams in the first place. While this seems an easily answerable issue in other jurisdictions, this is, unfortunately, a confusing proposition in the Philippines, despite a Supreme Court case alluding to the fact of employment and the application of a jurisprudential test indicating the presence of an employer-employee relationship. The confusion leads to further confusion in terms of the proper taxation of players, their government-mandated social security contributions, and their security of tenure.

Chapter 2. Sources of Employment Law

281. The Philippine Constitution is explicit in the country's policy to protect labor. It is a declared state policy to "affirm labor as a primary social economic force" and "protect the rights of workers and promote their welfare."[547] Further, the Constitution also states the following:

> SECTION 3. The State shall afford full protection to labor, local and overseas, organized and unorganized, and promote full employment and equality of employment opportunities for all.
> It shall guarantee the rights of all workers to self-organization, collective bargaining and negotiations, and peaceful concerted activities, including the right to strike in accordance with the law. They shall be entitled to security of tenure, humane conditions of work, and a living wage. They shall also participate in policy and decision-making processes affecting their rights and benefits as may be provided by law.
> The State shall promote the principle of shared responsibility between workers and employers and the preferential use of voluntary modes in settling disputes, including conciliation, and shall enforce their mutual compliance therewith to foster industrial peace.
> The State shall regulate the relations between workers and employers, recognizing the right of labor to its just share in the fruits of production and the right of enterprises to reasonable returns on investments, and to expansion and growth.[548]

282. The governing law for anything related to labor and employment is the Labor Code of the Philippines.[549] In fact, contracts of employment must comply with not only the Civil Code but also the Labor Code.[550] And in the situation where a labor contract complies with the Civil Code but not the Labor Code, the latter will prevail.[551]

---

547. Phil. Const. Art. 2, §18.
548. Phil. Const. Art. XIII, §3.
549. *See* Labor Code of the Philippines.
550. *Gopio v. Bautista*, G.R. No. 205953, Jun. 6, 2018. It states:

> Indeed, while our Civil Code recognizes that parties may stipulate in their contracts such terms and conditions as they may deem convenient, these terms and conditions must not be contrary to law, morals, good customs, public order or policy. The employment contract … is governed by Philippine labor laws. Hence, the stipulations, clauses, and terms and conditions of the contract must not contravene our labor law provisions.

551. *Ibid.* It states:

> Time and again, we have held that a contract of employment is imbued with public interest. The parties are not at liberty to insulate themselves and their relationships from the impact of labor laws and regulations by simply contracting with each other. Also, while a contract is the law between the parties, the provisions of positive law that regulate such contracts are deemed included and shall limit and govern the relations between the parties.

283. The Labor Code was issued as a presidential decree in 1974 by the dictator Ferdinand Marcos. While the Labor Code has seen its fair share of amendments in its more than four-decade existence, its underlying principles remain the same: protect labor, while still recognizing and respecting management prerogative. This tension is a common, if not the main, theme in most labor cases.

§1. Legal Status of Players and Employment Relationship

284. The fourfold test is the test of choice to determine whether an employer-employee relationship exists between parties.[552] This is the same test that will and should be used to determine the legal status of a player with his or her team. For an employer-employee relationship to arise, the following four elements must be present: first, the selection and engagement of the employee; second, the payment of wages; third, the power of dismissal over the employee; and fourth, the employer's power to control the employee's conduct.[553] The power of control has been considered the most important and most determinative.[554] If these four elements are not satisfied, then the hired party is most likely an independent contractor instead of an employee.

285. The author has always advocated the position that a professional player is, in fact, an employee of his or her team.[555] As will be discussed later, the four elements are present in the relationship between a player and his or her team. This position has been bolstered by a Supreme Court 2012 decision involving the illegal dismissal of a professional basketball player—the issue on dismissal a necessary implication that the player was treated and indeed an employee of his team. The said decision is worth discussing, as it is one of the few sports-related cases to reach the Supreme Court.

286. Negros Slashers, Inc. v. Alvin Teng ("Negros Slashers, Inc.")[556] involved the professional basketball team, Negros Slashers of the Metropolitan Basketball Association (the MBA has since closed shop) and basketball player, Alvin Teng. In 2000, his former MBA team, the Laguna Lakers, traded him to the Slashers. As a consequence of the trade, Teng executed a Player's Contract of Employment with the Slashers.[557]

---

552. *Manila Golf & Country Club Inc. v. IAC*, 237 SCRA 207 (1994); *Vinoya v. National Labor Relations Commission*, 324 SCRA 469 (2000); *Tan v. Lagraman*, 387 SCRA 393 (2002); *Francisco v. National Labor Relations Commission*, 500 SCRA 690 (2006).
553. *Orozco v. Fifth Division of the Court of Appeals*, 562 SCRA 36, 48 (2008).
554. *Ibid.*
555. Ignatius Michael D. Ingles, *Playing for Wages: Defining the Legal Relationship Between Professional Athlete and Team, a Sports Law Perspective on Philippine Labor Law*, 59 Ateneo L.J. 798, 805 (2014).
556. *See Negros Slashers Inc. v. Teng*, 666 SCRA 629 (2012).
557. *Ibid.*, at 632.

287. During a heated championship game in which he did not particularly play well, Teng was benched. Teng reacted to the benching by "[untying] his shoelaces and [donning] his practice jersey."[558] To make things worse, he called in sick for the next game.[559] The Slashers management terminated his contract because of his actions. In turn, Teng claimed he was illegally dismissed and filed a labor case with the Labor Arbiter (LA). The LA ruled for Teng, stating that he was illegally dismissed because the punishment was too harsh for his actions.

288. When the case reached the Supreme Court, the high court decided for the player and ruled that the Slashers illegally dismissed Teng. The Court called out Teng, even going so far as saying that his actions jeopardized the harmonious relationship he had with his teammates who undoubtedly felt abandoned by Teng's absence in the subsequent championship game.[560] Regardless of this finding, the Court found that his actions were not enough to merit the ultimate punishment of dismissal.[561] He was awarded PDP 2,530,000 in unpaid salaries, separation pay, and attorney's fees.[562]

289. Interestingly, the Supreme Court stated, "as an employee of the Negros Slashers, Teng was expected to work regularly"[563]—an acknowledgment of his employment status with the team. The fact that his contract was named a "Player's Contract of Employment" further bolstered the argument that he was indeed considered an employee of his team. Those who sit on the other side of the fence and consider professional athletes as independent contractors of their teams point to the fact that Teng's employment status was not raised as an issue of the case and, therefore, not binding as stare decisis. However, even if his employment status was at issue, applying the fourfold test will show that an employer-employee relationship does exist between a professional athlete and his or her team.

290. The first element of the fourfold test involves the selection and engagement of the player by the team. This is obviously present in sports teams and their athletes. In established leagues, such as the PBA, the selection and engagement are made through either a draft or free agency. In other leagues, this is done by simply offering a player a slot on the roster.

---

558. *Ibid.*
559. *Ibid.*, at 636.
560. *Ibid.*, at 642.
561. *Ibid.*, at 643.
562. *Ibid.*, at 644.
563. *Ibid.*, at 642.

291. The second element asks if athletes are paid by their teams. For professional athletes, this is answered by a resounding yes. PBA players are paid a maximum monthly salary of PDP 420,000.[564] Compared to other sports, the PBA salary is an outlier, with volleyball and football players earning considerably less than their professional basketball counterparts.

292. The high salary of basketball players has often raised the argument that they are independent contractors, with proponents of the view citing the Supreme Court case of a newscaster who was paid enormous amounts of pesos and was declared an independent contractor.[565] It seems a number of lawyers have equated the presence of high-paying wages to the absence of an employer-employee relationship. This, of course, is unfounded both in logic and law. If the premise were to be followed to its logical conclusion, then anyone lucky enough to have salaries would be automatically considered independent contractors—despite the fact that chief executive officers and other executives are considered employees, notwithstanding their seven-figure salaries. As to its basis in law, there lies the rub as well—neither the Labor Code nor jurisprudence states that the *amount* of wages plays a factor in the fourfold test.[566]

293. The third element is the power to dismiss a player. Part of this power is the power to discipline the players. This goes without saying and is self-explanatory. Teams definitely have the power to dismiss their players. And as to disciplining its players, professional teams in the Philippines have been known to fine and even suspend erring players.

294. The fourth element of control has always been the battleground when it comes to the recognition of players as employees. Proponents of the view that they are independent contractors would argue that teams do not have the power to control how a player actually plays the game. They would point to the fact that a team can no way control whether a player shoots with his left hand or kicks with her right foot or the technique he employs when throwing a curve ball. This, of course, is not the proper interpretation of the power of control.

295. The power of control has been defined to refer to the means and methods imposed by the employer to achieve results.[567] The Supreme Court has drawn a distinction between "rules that merely serve as guidelines towards the achievement of the mutually desired result without dictating the means or methods to be employed in attaining it, and those that control or fix the methodology and bind or restrict the party hired to the use of such means."[568] In the context of sports, these means or

564. Spin.ph, *How Much Can PBA Players Make in Terms of Bonuses? See Spin.ph Q&A*, https://www.spin.ph/basketball/pba/how-much-do-pba-players-make-in-terms-of-bonuses-read-spin-q- (Oct. 26, 2015).
565. *Sonza v. ABS-CBN Broadcasting Corp.*, 431 SCRA 583 (2004).
566. Ingles, *supra* note 555, at 800.
567. *Investment Planning Corp. of the Phil. v. Social Security System*, 21 SCRA 924, 929 (1967).
568. *Insular Life Assurance Co., Ltd. v. NLRC*, 179 SCRA 459, 465 (1989).

methods take the form of team philosophies and strategies that players must follow to achieve the "mutually desired result" of winning.

296. Control is also seen in an athlete's off-court or off-field obligations under his or her professional contract. Players are obliged to attend fan events, join every team trip, engage with members of the media, maintain a certain weight and physique, and even avoid certain activities that might expose them to injury or other risks. These are obligations and manifestations of control that even go beyond the means and methods imposed on a "normal" employee. It is indeed puzzling why the view that athletes are employees is not as widespread as it should be.

297. Control has and will never be interpreted to be control over the minutest of details in how an athlete actually plays the game. It has never been interpreted to include control over how a secretary takes down notes or how a cook fries an egg or a janitor mops the floor, as this interpretation would obviously be logically absurd.[569] Yet, arguments to this effect persist in the Philippine legal landscape, mainly because of ignorance of the employment status of professional athletes in other jurisdictions and sadly, because some teams simply refuse to give their players the benefits granted by law to employees.

298. The proper characterization of the employment status of athletes is important, as it comes with a host of legal implications. The first of which involves the benefits they will be entitled to as employees, such as employer-mandated contributions to the player's Social Security System account.[570] The second revolves around the player's tax liabilities. As mentioned in the section on taxation, player-employees are not subject to VAT because services rendered under an employer-employee relationship are exempt from VAT.[571] Player-employees also do not have to worry about filing their returns with the BIR, as income earners under an employer-employee relationship qualify for substituted filing by their employees—this significantly reduces the risk of audit which independent contractors face when they file and compute their own tax liabilities.

299. The more significant implications revolve around two fundamental rights of employees: the security of tenure and the right to enter into unions and collectively bargain. Both are discussed below.

300. The Labor Code guarantees the security of tenure to employees. More specifically, the Labor Code enumerates the only instances when an employer may legally dismiss an employee. These have been grouped quite conveniently into two: authorized and just causes.

569. Ingles, *supra* note 555, at 802.
570. *Ibid.*, at 807.
571. *Ibid.*

301. Authorized causes involve employer-initiated reasons for termination, such as redundancy or serious business losses.[572] For example, a professional team which will close shop due to business losses is authorized to release its players, as the law acknowledges that it cannot compel a business to stay open.[573] Employees terminated due to authorized causes are entitled to separation pay, the amounts of which differ depending on the reason for termination.

302. Just causes are more applicable to professional teams and athletes, as these are causes that allow a team to dismiss a player due to his or her actions. Players who are terminated based on just causes are not entitled to separation pay, for the simple reason that the termination was their fault, to begin with. The Labor Code enumerates the just causes as follows: engaging in serious misconduct, willful disobedience of lawful orders of the employer, gross and habitual neglect of one's duties, committing fraud against the teams in connection with an employee's duties, willful betrayal of trust, committing a crime against the person of the employer or his or her immediate family, and other acts analogous to the enumeration.[574]

303. On top of the enumerated just causes, employers are also allowed to terminate employees based on reasonable and lawful grounds specified under company policies.[575] Hence, it is valid to terminate a player on account of match-fixing or gambling as long as these are specified in either the employment contract or the team policies. Weight has also been considered a bona fide occupational qualification in a case involving a plus-sized flight attendant.[576] Hence, it will most likely be valid to dismiss a player who has repeatedly failed to reach the fitness levels required by his or her sport. The emphasis should be on the word "repeatedly," as the Supreme Court has constantly ruled that dismissal should be the last resort in dealing with an erring employee.[577]

304. Certain laws and cases have prohibited employers from using certain discriminatory reasons to terminate employees. For example, employers are not allowed to require as a condition of employment or continued employment that a woman employee shall not get married.[578] Pregnancy or the number of children a woman has is also not a valid ground for terminating an employment contract.[579] Compulsory HIV testing (or testing players without consent) as a precondition to employment or continued employment is likewise illegal.[580] These will squarely apply to professional teams as well.

---

572. Labor Code of the Philippines, Arts. 298–299.
573. *Ibid.*
574. *Ibid.*, Art. 297.
575. Rules to Implement the Labor Code *as amended*, Book VI, Rule 1-A, §6 (DOLE).
576. *See Yrasuegui v. Philippine Airlines Inc.*, 569 SCRA 467 (2008).
577. Negros Slashers, *supra* note 556 at 643.
578. Labor Code of the Philippines, Art. 134.
579. The Responsible Parenthood and Reproductive Health Act of 2012, Republic Act No. 10354, §23(c) (2012).
580. Philippine AIDS Prevention and Control Act of 1998, Republic Act No. 8504, §7 (1998).

305. Despite the existence of a just cause to terminate an employee, the law has been consistent that an employer must still follow the proper process in firing the employee. More popularly known as the two-notice rule, employers must first give employees a written notice informing them of the violations allegedly committed and a chance to explain their side. After they explain their side, the employer must then issue another written notice explaining the findings and the decision to terminate.[581] Even if the termination is completely justified, employers may still be held liable for damages if they fail to follow the two-notice rule.[582]

306. If a player feels he or she has been unjustly terminated, mediation will first be conducted by a Single Entry Approach Desk Officer (SEADO) in the Department of Labor and Employment (DOLE).[583] If, after a series of conferences, things have not been settled between the player and a team, the case will be referred to a LA who will then rule on the issue.[584] Parties unhappy with the decision of the LA can appeal the case all the way up to the Supreme Court if they choose to.

307. A player who is ruled to have been illegally dismissed is entitled to backwages and reinstatement to the team. However, if reinstatement is impossible due to the strained relations between the player and the team, the player will be given separation pay instead.[585] Backwages include the player's salary for the unexpired portion of the contract and other benefits that he or she may be entitled to.[586]

§2. Athlete Unionization and Other Options

308. The right to form a union is also an important by-product of the employment status of professional athletes. The Philippine Constitution guarantees the right of all workers to self-organization, collective bargaining and negotiations, and peaceful concerted activities, including the right to strike in accordance with the law.[587] The Constitution states, "the right of the people, including those employed in the public and private sectors, to form unions, associations, or societies for purposes not contrary to law shall not be abridged."[588] And to add emphasis, it also "affirms labor as a primary social economic force and shall protect the rights of workers and promote their welfare."[589]

309. The Labor Code has operationalized this constitutional mandate by giving the "right to self-organization and to form, join or assist labor organizations of their

581. *JAKA Food Processing Corporation v. Pacot,* 454 SCRA 119, 123 (2005).
582. *Ibid.,* at 124.
583. The Rules of Procedure of the Single Entry Approach (SEnA), DOLE DO No. 107 (DOLE, Feb. 25, 2011).
584. Labor Code of the Philippines, Art. 228.
585. *See Torillo v. Leogardo Jr.*, 197 SCRA 471, 477 (1991).
586. *See St. Louis College of Tuguegarao v. NLRC*, 177 SCRA 151 (1989).
587. Phil. Const. Art. XIII, §3.
588. Phil. Const. Art. III, §8.
589. Phil. Const. Art. II, §18.

own choosing for purposes of collective bargaining" to all employees, regardless of industry and for-profit nature.[590] Those who are self-employed and those whose work is intermittent in nature may not form unions, but they can form labor organizations for the purpose of enhancing and defending their interests and for their mutual aid and protection.[591]

310. While public policy points to the formation and protection of unions, actually forming a union may prove difficult for professional athletes.[592] Note that unions of professional athletes in other countries like the U.S. (say, for example, the National Basketball Players Association) are league-wide unions, with players of different teams in one single and unified union. Current Philippine laws and the structure of professional leagues pose significant challenges to creating these league-wide unions.[593]

311. The main challenge is determining the appropriate collective bargaining unit (CBU), which the union will represent. Said CBU must be appropriate, which will be determined by the interests of its members.[594] The problem lies in the doctrine that unions have to be employee-based, i.e., "two different employers make two different unions."[595] And as players are employees of their respective teams, CBUs will necessarily be team based, which will thus lead to unions based per team—not a league-wide union that will be the ideal vehicle to ushering in league-wide change.[596]

312. If professional athletes wish to create a league-wide union, it will have to be under the aegis of multiemployer bargaining.[597] This will allow different "mini-unions" to come together to bargain with the various employer-teams in the league, with the goal of having a collective bargaining agreement (CBA) that will bind everyone in the league.[598] This, of course, will be hard to achieve, given the conditions set by law.

313. First, only legitimate labor unions which are also the incumbent exclusive bargaining agents may join.[599] Second, only employers with their counterpart labor unions may join.[600] If a team does not have an existing union, then it may not join the discussions—a fact that will immediately disrupt the hopes of a league-wide

---

590. Labor Code of the Philippines, Art. 253.
591. *Ibid.*
592. Ignatius Michael D. Ingles & Katrina Bianca Louise S. Diploma, *Strength in Unity: Reviving the PBA Union*, 43 Ateneo L. J. 689, 705 (2019).
593. *Ibid.*
594. Cesario Alvero Azucena Jr., *Everyone's Labor Code*, 304 (9th ed. 2018).
595. *Ibid.*
596. Ingles & Diploma, *supra* note 592.
597. Rules to Implement the Labor Code, Book V, Rule XVI, §5.
598. *Ibid.*
599. *Ibid.*
600. *Ibid.*

CBA. Third, employers *must* consent to the entire process.[601] It is not hard to imagine an employer-team or two holding out to prevent a league-wide CBA, especially given the condition and politics surrounding Philippine professional sports.[602]

314. The bleak outlook for unions and league-wide CBAs notwithstanding, the law does provide for other avenues for players to unite to protect their own interests. Another way is the creation of the workers' association.[603] Workers' associations are organizations established for the mutual aid and protection of their members or for any legitimate purpose *other* than collective bargaining.[604] While associations for mutual aid and protection are *not* allowed to enter into collective bargaining (and thus precluding negotiations for CBAs), they can still work to protect players' rights and deal with teams and the league.[605] These workers' associations can be formed under the Labor Code or even as non-stock, non-profit corporations under the Revised Corporation Code (RCC) of the Philippines.

315. The players' association has one key advantage over unions: the existence of the employer-employee relationship is not mandatory to form these associations.[606] This, in a way, solves the problem of players in a league having different employers. Players can band together, despite having different employers.[607]

316. The disadvantages, however, are quite significant.[608] First, a players' association cannot compel teams to negotiate for a CBA, as it is explicitly prohibited from doing so. Without the legal duty to bargain in good faith, negotiations between a players' association and the different teams will be founded on goodwill and consent.[609] Second, a players' association is left without perhaps one of the strongest weapon in labor relations—the power to strike. Under Philippine law, only unions have the right to strike.[610] Without the said power to strike, a players' association loses a helpful tool for leverage.[611]

317. Despite these disadvantages, a players' association may be a good place to start to show a unified front; its collective voice may just be the moral pressure needed to advocate change.[612] Retired basketball players currently have an association to advocate for their rights and protection; the Samahan ng mga Dating Professional na Basketbolista Foundation[613]has organized fundraising events to help

601. *Ibid.*
602. Ingles & Diploma, *supra* note 592, at 710.
603. Labor Code of the Philippines, Art. 253.
604. Rules to Implement the Labor Code, Book V, Rule I, s. 1 (ccc).
605. Ingles & Diploma, *supra* note 592, at 719.
606. *Samahan ng Manggagagawa sa Hanjin Shipyard v. Bureau of Labor Relations*, 772 SCRA 613, 629 (2015).
607. Ingles & Diploma, *supra* note 592, at 719–720.
608. *Ibid.*, at 720.
609. *Ibid.*
610. Cesario Alvero Azucena Jr., *The Labor Code with Comments and Cases Vol. II*, 579 (2016).
611. Ingles & Diploma, *supra* note 592, at 720.
612. *Ibid.*
613. Roughly translates to "Retired Professional Basketball Players Association."

retired basketball players. Fédération Internationale des Associations de Footballeurs Professionnels (FIFPro) had its own local organization to protect Filipino football players—the Filipino Professional Footballers Association is supported by FIFPro Asia. This seems to have suffered a quiet and untimely demise.

§3. Employment Disputes

318. Employment disputes are likewise governed by the Labor Code and are settled under the ambit and jurisdiction of the National Labor Relations Commission (NLRC). The NLRC is a quasi-judicial agency attached to the DOLE which is mandated to adjudicate and settle labor and management disputes in the Philippines.[614] The variety of employment issues that the LA and the NLRC may rule upon are vast. These include termination disputes, money claims and claims for damages arising from employer-employee relations, and the claims arising from the breach of law-mandated work standards.[615] Decisions by the LA are generally appealable to the NLRC.[616]

319. While the LA can be seen as the first instance adjudicatory authority in labor cases, the state policy mandates that conciliation meetings first be conducted to attempt to settle controversies in an amicable manner. This state policy is manifested and embodied in the implementation of the Single Entry Approach (SEnA). The SEnA is essentially a one-stop shop for aggrieved employees who may simply fill up a form with an itemized list of usual complaints against employers.[617] The SEADO is normally available to help with filling out the Form. The SEADO will then schedule a series of conferences between the employees and the team or employer to work things out. Personal appearance is a must in these conferences.[618] While a lawyer is not required in these instances, employees may bring a lawyer along for advice or support.[619]

320. If things are not settled at the level of the SEnA, then the case will be referred to the LA for another bout of mandatory conciliation and mediation conferences. If these still do not work out, then the LA will conduct a full-blown hearing. The procedure in the LA is not as strict as the procedure adopted in the regular courts. In fact, the 2011 NLRC Rules of Procedure explicitly state that these proceedings are non-litigious in nature.[620] The technical rules of court do not apply, and the LA may avail of all reasonable means to settle the matter.[621] This pronouncement notwithstanding, there is still a modicum of formality and strictness in these LA hearings where the issuance of summons and the submission of position papers

614. Labor Code of the Philippines, Art. 224.
615. *Ibid.*, Art. 224(a)(1)-(6).
616. *Ibid.*, Art. 224(c).
617. The Rules of Procedure of the Single Entry Approach (SEnA).
618. *Ibid.*, §3(a).
619. *Ibid.*, §3(b).
620. 2011 NLRC Rules of Procedure, Rule V, §2 (NLRC, May 31, 2011).
621. *Ibid.*

and pleadings are still required. Decisions of the LA may be an appeal to the NLRC, whose decisions, in turn, may be appealed to the Court of Appeals and finally to the Supreme Court.

321. The usual tactic of employers in these cases is to deny the employer-employee relationship altogether and claim the lack of jurisdiction of the LA and NLRC. For example, certain teams may argue that their player or their coach or whoever in their roster is engaged under an independent contractor relationship. In such cases, the LA and the NLRC can rule on their own jurisdiction. And in the event that it does agree that it does not have any jurisdiction, it will dismiss the case. Under such circumstances, the proper mode of dispute resolution would be under the regular court system.

§4. Foreign Employees and Immigration Issues

322. One of the aspects of professional sports that excites fans is the influx of foreign athletes to bolster teams. Colloquially called "imports," these foreign athletes have always been the stuff of legend and fandom in sporting circles, particularly in the PBA. American basketball players have long come to the sunny shores of the Philippines to strut their stuff. Some imports have even transitioned to call the Philippines their home, with the likes of Norman Black opting to stay and coach both at the collegiate and professional level after successful stints as a PBA import. Others have chosen to briefly stay but leave indelible marks in the local basketball culture, such as the legendary NBA player Billy Ray Bates who was said to have lifted a Volkswagen Beetle to show his fitness and strength to his local coach (on top of his 46.2 points per game average) and the incomparable Tony Harris who scored 105 points in a basketball game in 1992.[622]

323. Other leagues have sought foreign athletes to up the ante of their respective competitions. Both the PFL, PSL, and PVL have allowed foreign athletes to suit up for their teams. There are a number of players from different countries in Africa who have suited up for football teams in the PFL, while North and South American volleyball players have bolstered teams in the PSL and PVL. It goes without saying that teams must comply with the required immigration and labor laws before these players can suit up and showcase their talents.

324. The legal requirements depend on how long the imports will play in the Philippines. For those who will not stay for more than six months, they can apply for a Special Work Permit (SWP) with the Bureau of Immigration (BI). The SWP allows non-resident foreigner athletes, trainers, coaches, and participants to engage in their respective sports for engagements less than six months. An SWP can be

622. Gerry Ramos, *Does Having an NBA-Caliber Import Guarantee a PBA Title? Let's See,* Spin.ph, https://www.spin.ph/life/guide/nba-caliber-imports-who-played-in-pba-a793-20190812-lfrm2 (Aug. 12, 2019).

applied for with the BI by filling out the application form and completing the documentary requirements. The SWP is non-extendible, so if these non-resident foreigners go over the six-month limit, an AEP and a 9g visa will be required.[623]

325. For those who will play and stay here for more than six months, an AEP from DOLE must be secured, as well as a Pre-Arranged Employee Commercial Visa, more popularly known as the 9g visa. The AEP is a document issued by the DOLE that authorizes a foreign national to work in the Philippines.[624] The AEP and 9g visa are employer-specific.[625] Hence, a change in employers—such as what would happen in a trade of a player or termination and subsequent rehiring of a foreign coach—would require some hoop-jumping in order to maintain legal status in the Philippines.[626] While the AEP and 9g visa are being processed, local employers can apply for a Provisional Work Permit (PWP) in order for the foreign employee to start working. The PWP lasts for three months or until the 9g visa is issued, whichever comes earlier.

326. The AEP must be applied for with the DOLE Regional Office or Field Office having jurisdiction over the intended place of work. The documentary requirements are needed to apply for the AEP on the DOLE website. Among these requirements is the contract of employment with the Filipino employer. One of the substantial conditions in the release of the AEP is the prior determination of the non-availability of a person in the Philippines who is competent, able, and willing to perform the same services which the foreigner will be engaged to do.[627] AEPs are required for non-resident foreigners[628] and not those who legally reside in the Philippines.

327. The validity of the American basketball coach, Tim Cone's AEP, made it all the way to the Supreme Court in 1991.[629] In that case, the BCAP questioned Tim Cone's AEP arguing that there was no showing there that was another person in the Philippines who was competent, able, and willing to perform the services required

623. Rules Governing the Issuance of Special Work Permit (SWP), Provisional Permit to Work (PPW), and Pre-Arranged Employment Visa Under Section 9(G) of the Philippine Immigration Act of 1940 (PIA), as Amended, Memorandum Circular No. AFF- 05-001 (Bureau of Immigration, Mar. 18, 2005).
624. Department of Labor and Employment, *Frequently Asked Questions on the Revised Rules for the Issuance of Employment Permits to Foreign Nationals (D.O. No. 97-09)*, http://www.ble.dole.gov.ph/index.php/web-pages/118-alien-employment-permit (last visited May 17, 201 8).
625. Anna Carmi Calsado-Amoroso & Patrick Edward L. Balisong, *In or Out: Gaps in Philippine Immigration Law in Relation to Foreign Athletes and Sports Leagues Regulations—Migration and Human Rights Issues,* 63 Ateneo L. J. 689, 799 (2019).
626. *Ibid.*
627. Labor Code of the Philippines, Art. 40 (1974).
628. Department of Labor and Employment, *supra* note 624.
629. *General Milling Corp.,* 273 Phil.

of Tim Cone.[630] The Supreme Court agreed with BCAP and ruled against Cone and his employer, resulting in the cancelation of his AEP.[631]

328. Cone, however, has since been allowed to coach in the Philippines, much to the delight of basketball fans who continue to marvel at his penchant for sticking to the triangle offense. Cone is married to a Filipina, which makes him a permanent resident under section 13(a) of the Philippine Immigration Act of 1940, and therefore, outside the ambit of the AEP.

329. Recently, an odd trend has started and is catching on that seems to skirt and circumvent the AEP requirement. Local teams, wary of the Tim Cone decision, have resorted to contracting coaches and simply calling them "basketball consultants." As they are not considered coaches and employees of the team, they argue that no AEP is thereafter needed. In truth, these "basketball consultants" act as head coaches, except on paper. This has been the preferred tactic of certain professional teams and even a university team. It seems only a matter of time before this is questioned.

330. The 9g visa allows foreigners entering the Philippines to work here and earn compensation. Employers must apply for the 9g visa with the BI on behalf of their foreign employees. A requirement for the issuance of a 9g visa is the personal appearance of the would-be employee at a hearing in the BI. After, an Alien Certificate of Registration I-Card (ACR I-Card) will be issued to the foreign employee. This ACR I-Card must be presented to immigration officers every time these foreigners travel outside the Philippines, lest they are barred entry into the Philippines after a brief sojourn abroad for vacation or whatever reason.

630. *Ibid.*
631. *Ibid.,* at 220.

Part III. Doping and Sport

Chapter 1. General Issues

331. The Philippine National Anti-Doping Organization (PHI-NADO) heads anti-doping education in the country. Established by the PSC as an independent organization, the PHI-NADO is the country's accredited anti-doping organization under World Anti-Doping Agency (WADA) and the South East Asian Regional Anti-doping Organization. Since its inception, it has been conducting seminars throughout the country on the dangers and pitfalls of doping. While anti-doping education has been regularly conducted for athletes who participate internationally, doping was only just thrust into the public consciousness and awareness in 2018 when basketball star, Kiefer Isaac Ravena, was sanctioned by FIBA for prohibited substances.

332. Ravena played for the Philippine national basketball team during the FIBA Basketball World Cup 2019 qualifiers.[632] After the February 25, 2018 game against Japan in Manila, FIBA conducted an in-competition doping test on Ravena.[633] During the test, Ravena did not disclose any supplements he had been taking on his doping control form.[634] His sample was then sent to the WADA-accredited laboratory in Montreal, Canada.[635] Unfortunately for Ravena, the lab test report revealed the presence of methylhexaneamine, dimethylbutylamine, and higenamine, all specified substances under the WADA 2018 Prohibited List.[636]

333. Ravena then requested for the analysis of the B Sample, a right granted to him by WADA rules.[637] The B sample, however, confirmed the findings of the A sample.[638] This prompted FIBA to charge him with an anti-doping rule violation under Article 2.1 of its Internal Regulations governing Anti-doping (FIBA ADR).[639]

632. Decision, FIBA Disciplinary Panel established in accordance with Art. 8.1 of the FIBA Internal Regulations Governing Anti-Doping in the matter Kiefer Isaac Ravena, p. 1 (May 22, 2018), https://news.abs-cbn.com/focus/05/28/18/read-fiba-timeline-of-kiefer-ravena-testing-results-suspension.
633. *Ibid.*
634. *Ibid.*
635. *Ibid.*, p. 2.
636. *Ibid.*
637. *Ibid.*
638. *Ibid.*
639. *Ibid.*, p. 3.

In turn, SBP, the country's NSA for basketball, sent FIBA a letter seeking leniency for Ravena, stating that Ravena wished to embark on an "educational drive regarding anti-doping."[640]

334. In his two written statements, Ravena noted that he had taken a workout drink called DUST, which he had purchased in Australia after his usual workout drink ran out.[641] He claimed that the retail representative who had sold him DUST stated that it was similar to his usual workout drink.[642] He likewise stated that it was an honest mistake that he had not indicated the drink in his doping control form and that he had no intention to cheat. He also said that he did not have any formal anti-doping education and did not research or know that DUST contained banned substances.[643]

335. The FIBA Disciplinary Panel decided to suspend Ravena for eighteen months, from February 25, 2018, to August 24, 2019.[644] It found that Ravena did indeed commit an anti-doping rule violation because of the presence of the prohibited substances in his system.[645] The Panel found that the ingestion of the prohibited substances was intentional under the FIBA ADR.[646] It, however, reduced the period of ineligibility from the FIBA ADR's mandated two-year period to eighteen months because Ravena established the source of the prohibited substances and a number of other circumstances.[647] The Panel noted that Ravena did not know DUST contained prohibited substances and that he had never received any anti-doping education prior to the incident.[648] However, the Panel stated that Ravena should have at least performed an internet search on DUST before taking it. Interestingly, the Panel stated that his lack of anti-doping education did not exonerate him from liability but found that it contributed to his wrong perception of the risk involved in taking supplements.[649]

336. Ravena did not appeal the decision and served his period of ineligibility with prudence. As mandated by the FIBA ADR, he steered away from any basketball-related activity and focused on a nationwide anti-doping education campaign instead. As the ineligibility covered any and all basketball-related activities, he sat out the remainder of the PBA season and the rest of the Philippines' FIBA World Cup qualifiers.

337. The Ravena case made national headlines, especially because of Ravena's storied collegiate career in the UAAP, his regular stint with the national basketball

---

640. *Ibid.*
641. *Ibid.*
642. *Ibid.*
643. *Ibid.*
644. *Ibid.*, p. 4.
645. *Ibid.*
646. *Ibid.*, p. 6.
647. *Ibid.*, p. 10.
648. *Ibid.*, p. 9.
649. *Ibid.*

team, and his impressive start to his career in the PBA with his team, the NLEX Road Warriors. It also shone the spotlight on the glaring lack of anti-doping education in the country. People opined that Ravena was a drug addict, wrongly equating WADA prohibited substances with illegal drug use under the country's antidrug laws. Since then, the PSC has upped its efforts in anti-doping education, with the aforementioned PHI-NADO leading the cause.

338. While the new vigor for anti-doping education is commendable, the actual implementation of anti-doping mechanisms is still an ongoing question. The efforts of PHI-NADO have to be bolstered by the participation of private sports organizations and associations. It remains to be seen if leagues and associations like the PBA, the UAAP, the PFL, or the NCAA actually do conduct doping tests or at the very least capable of doing so. Note that the drug tests conducted by GAB for the release of a professional license seem to test only for the presence of marijuana or meth in the system of a prospective license holder.[650]

650. Games and Amusements Board, Status Update, *Clarification from the Games and Amusement Board* (Jan. 6, 2017), https://www.facebook.com/GamesandAmusementsBoard/photos/pcb.1517528191677934/1517527298344690/?type=3&theater (last visited May 17, 2018).

Part IV. Sport and Commerce

Chapter 1. General Issues

339. The growing popularity of sports has been accompanied by the steady growth of the sports business industry. Businesses have tapped athletes, both professional and amateur, as worthwhile endorsers. Collegiate sports have seen a steady influx of corporate sponsors, particularly in UAAP basketball and volleyball. Businesses have also used professional leagues, such as the PBA, the PVL, and the PSL as vehicles to build brand awareness, as teams in these leagues are not only backed by corporate sponsors but also carry brands as their actual team names. For example, the most popular PBA team, Barangay Ginebra San Miguel, is named after Ginebra San Miguel, a local gin, while PVL champions, the Creamline Cool Smashers, gets its name from the dairy product line of its sponsor, Republic Biscuit Corporation.

340. The monetization of sports has also been seen in various media outlets. Two local TV networks have exerted great effort to be the leading voice in sports. ABS-CBN established its Sports and Action channel, which broadcasts UAAP games to the delight of Filipinos worldwide. Not to be outdone, TV5 carries the ESPN brand (with the local equivalent of SportsCenter) and the PBA. Sports coverage has, of course, spilled over to the internet, with each media outlet having its fair share of streaming services for sports.

341. With that said, even the increasing amount of money funneled into anything sports has not pushed Congress to make sports-specific laws for businesses. As such, general business laws will apply to anyone who wishes to wet their beak in the sports industry. These laws are discussed below.

Chapter 2. Public Regulation

§1. Constitutional Restrictions and Foreign Ownership

342. Mass media is regulated by none other than the Philippine Constitution. Well aware of the importance of media in influencing citizens, the framers of the Constitution imposed strict guidelines for both the ownership and management of mass media. Frankly put, mass media companies must be 100% owned and managed by Filipinos.[651] The Constitution leaves no room for foreign participation. Hence, foreign mass media companies, particularly those with a leaning or specialization in sports, will have to find other ways to penetrate the Philippine market. These can include licensing or franchising agreements with a Filipino partner.

343. Violation of this constitutional restriction brings a whole host of headaches, the least of which is the suspension or revocation of a license to operate with the Securities and Exchange Commission (SEC). Of course, the underlying question that must be answered is what types of media fall within the constitutional purview of "mass media." Admittedly, the Constitution was drafted, signed, and ratified in an era of print and television. Hence, there are those who argue that digital media was not contemplated by the Constitution and is, therefore, exempt from the ownership and management restriction. However, both the SEC and the Department of Justice have given "mass media" a broader meaning to include "any medium of communication designed to reach the masses,"[652] which would necessarily include digital media in all its forms. Internet businesses, however, are excluded from the meaning of mass media.[653]

344. This constitutional restriction was put to a head in 2017 and 2018 when the SEC questioned the ownership structure of Rappler.com, a news outlet that operates exclusively online. The controversy raised questions whether online news outlets are included in the meaning of "mass media" and whether the issuance of Philippine Depository Receipts to foreign companies, as what Rappler.com had issued to Omidyar Network, are indicative of foreign ownership.[654] Foreign mass media investors who wish to tap the Philippine sports market through "newer" forms of media will do well to navigate the tricky maze caused by the said foreign ownership restriction.

345. Aside from ownership restrictions, sports broadcast businesses must also obtain a primary franchise from Congress. Under the Constitution, public utilities like broadcast stations require legislative franchises which last for a maximum

651. Phil. Const. Art. XVI, §11(1).
652. SEC-OGC Opinion No. 14-06 Re: Marketing and Sale of Digital Publication through the Internet and Mobile Technology; Advertising; Mass Media (SEC, May 8, 2014).
653. *Ibid.*
654. Rappler, *FAQs: Rappler's SEC Case,* https://www.rappler.com/about-rappler/about-us/194165-frequently-asked-questions-rappler-sec-case (Jan. 28, 2018).

period of fifty years.[655] In practice, these legislative franchises are granted for twenty-five years, subject to renewal. The requirement puts broadcast stations at the mercy of Congress, which can flex their political muscle if it so chooses—as it has done with the franchise renewal of ABS-CBN.[656] Upon obtaining the primary franchise, it must then seek authorization from the National Telecommunications Commission (NTC) for a secondary license. If the NTC finds everything in order, it will issue a Certificate of Public Convenience and Necessity and the broadcast business will be on its way to making its TV or radio station operational.

346. Other forms of sports media, such as those offered online or digitally, do not need this two-step franchise requirement. This is a welcome note for those exploring internet-based dissemination of sports information, such as podcasts, sports-specific blogs, and websites. The same can be said about print media, as newspapers and magazines have historically been exempted from the requirement of Congressional licensing for free speech reasons.

347. Speaking of foreign ownership restrictions, the President regularly issues the Foreign Investment Negative List. The Negative List serves as a helpful guide for foreigners looking to invest in the Philippines. The latest version of the Negative List was issued on October 29, 2018.[657] For industries outside the list, foreigners can wholly own the business. Relevant to sports are the following excerpts from the Negative List (Table 4).

Table 4 Foreign Ownership Restrictions

No Foreign Equity	*Up to 40% Foreign Equity Allowed*
(1) Mass media, except recording and internet business or internet access providers. (2) Retail trade enterprises with paid-up capital of less than USD 2,500,000. (3) Ownership, operation, and management of cockpits.	(1) Ownership of private lands. (2) Operation of public utilities, except power generation and the supply of electricity. (3) Educational institutions, with a few exceptions. (4) Saunas, bathhouses, massage clinics and other like activities regulated by law for public moral purposes, except wellness centers. (5) All forms of gambling, except those covered by investment agreements with PAGCOR. (6) Domestic market enterprises with paid-in equity capital of less than the equivalent of USD 200,000.

655. Phil. Const. Art. XII, §11.
656. Michelle Abad, *Timeline: Duterte Against ABS-CBN's Franchise Renewal*, Rappler (Jan. 17, 2020), https://www.rappler.com/newsbreak/iq/249550-timeline-duterte-against-abs-cbn-franchise-renewal.
657. Promulgating the Eleventh Regular Foreign Investment Negative List, Executive Order 65 (2018).

348. Foreign retailers who wish to establish a presence in the Philippines have to comply with the Retail Trade Liberalization Act of 2000 (RTLA).[658] Under the RTLA, foreigners may wholly own retail businesses in one of either two ways. The paid-up capital must be at least USD 7,500,000 provided the investments for establishing a store is at least USD 830,000, or the foreign investor specializes in high-end or luxury products with a paid-up capital of USD 250,000 per store.[659] High-end products refer to "goods which are not necessary for life maintenance and whose demand is generated in large part by the higher income groups."[660]

349. Foreign investors must also be aware of the Anti-Dummy Law.[661] Passed in 1936, while the Philippines was still under American law, the law has survived the test of time and prohibits the use of "dummy arrangements" to circumvent foreign ownership restrictions. Anyone caught violating the Anti-Dummy Law faces jail time of up to fifteen years.[662]

§2. Sports Businesses

350. Sports businesses can generally choose between three options to conduct operations: the sole proprietorship, the partnership, and the corporation. Registration requirements will differ for each.

351. Sole proprietors are required to register with the Department of Trade and Industry (DTI). This is a fairly easy process, which begins by registering the desired business name online. Sole proprietorships have been the vehicle of choice for small- and medium-business owners (such as neighborhood basketball jersey manufacturers) because of the relative ease involved in the registration. The downside is that sole proprietorships do not limit the liability of the entrepreneurs, as there is no separate juridical entity created in the registration of sole proprietorships.[663] Thus, sole proprietors are exposed to personal liability for the debts incurred in their businesses.

352. Partnerships are governed by the Civil Code and are created when "two or more persons bind themselves together to contribute to a common fund with the intention of dividing profits among themselves."[664] Partnerships are often chosen by

658. Retail Trade Liberalization Act of 2000, Republic Act No. 8762 (2000).
659. *Ibid.*, §5.
660. *Ibid.*
661. An Act to Punish Acts of Evasion of the Laws on the Nationalization of Certain Rights, Franchises or Privileges, Commonwealth Act No. 108 (1936).
662. *Ibid.*, §1.
663. *Jariol Jr. v. Sandiganbayan,* 188 SCRA 475, 489 (1990).
664. Civil Code of the Philippines, Art. 1767.

entrepreneurs who wish to keep the business within themselves, as interest in partnerships is generally non-transferrable.[665] While the mere agreement of partners gives rise to the creation of a separate juridical entity, partnerships must still be registered with the SEC.

353. Corporations are the most popular vehicles for sports businesses, particularly because of their structural integrity and the limited liability of their shareholders. As separate juridical entities, corporations shield their shareholders from personal liability, allowing a greater avenue for risk-taking in businesses. Foreign sports businesses, such as Nike and Adidas, have established local subsidiaries to build their brands in the Philippines, while their local counterparts (such as World Balance) have also used corporations to carry out their businesses. Corporations must be registered with the SEC, and only upon registration is it granted existence by operation of law.

354. In 2019, the RCC was enacted under Republic Act No. 11232, giving some long-awaited changes to the thirty-eight-year-old Corporation Code. One of the highlights is the creation of the One Person Corporation (OPC), which, as its name suggests, is a corporation with a single stockholder.[666] The OPC has been touted as a viable alternative to sole proprietorships because of the limited liability feature and the no-minimum capital requirement.[667] Whether sole proprietors will make the jump to OPCs remains to be seen. Another change ushered in by the RCC is the removal of the fifty-year limit on corporate life. Corporations can now last perpetually,[668] adding even more stability.

355. Aside from the registration requirements with the DTI or the SEC, businesses must also register with the local government where they operate and other government agencies. Businesses must coordinate closely with their respective local governments like cities or municipalities in order to obtain a business permit to operate. Thereafter, these businesses must also register with the BIR for tax purposes and the Social Security System, Philippine Health Insurance Corporation, and the Home Development Mutual Fund for mandatory employee benefits and contributions.

§3. Sports Agencies

356. One of the enterprises benefitting from the growing popularity of amateur and professional sports is the sports agency. More and more sports agencies have popped up in the recent few years, particularly due to the rise of social media as another avenue for monetization. These sports agencies serve as useful go-betweens for influencer-athletes and businesses who seek mileage on social media. Some of

665. *Ibid.*, Art. 1804.
666. Revised Corporation Code of the Philippines, Republic Act No. 11232, §116 (2019).
667. *Ibid.*, §§117, 130.
668. *Ibid.*, §11.

the bigger sports agencies have concentrated their efforts on the amateur scene, keeping rosters of collegiate athletes at their beck and call.

357. Unlike other jurisdictions, the Philippines does not have a special law geared toward sports agents and sports agencies. Instead, any agency relationship is governed by the Civil Code of the Philippines. Under the Civil Code, a contract of agency occurs when "a person binds himself to render some service or do something in representation or on behalf of another, with the consent of the latter."[669] It is valid and binding by mere consent and does not require any form. As long as both the agent and the athlete agree on the basic aspect of representation, then an agency relationship is perfected.[670] The contract of agency may even be oral[671] unless the law specifies otherwise, such as when the sale of immovable property such as land is involved.[672] There is likewise no law or association rule that prohibits amateurs or student-athletes from securing the services of an agent.

358. The general legal obligation of a sports agent is to act within his or her scope of authority.[673] To this end, the agent may perform acts to achieve the purpose of the agency, which is often the opening up of endorsement opportunities for the athlete-client. Naturally, the agent must act according to the instructions of the client.[674]

359. On the side of the client, he or she is bound to comply with all the obligations that the agent had contracted within the scope of authority.[675] However, obligations entered into by the agent *beyond* his or her authority do not bind the principal[676] unless the principal chooses to ratify such unauthorized action.[677] Another instance when the client-athlete may still be bound for an unauthorized act of the agent is under the doctrine of apparent authority. In such case, when an agent acts in excess of authority, the principal may still be bound if he or she manifests the existence of an agency and a third person relies on the conduct of the principal.[678]

360. The agent is liable for the damages which, through his or her non-performance, the client-athlete may suffer.[679] In the absence of instructions on how to carry on the agency, the agent must be diligent and act as a good father would do.[680] Agents must also not perform acts that would result in loss or damage to the

669. Civil Code of the Philippines, Art. 1868.
670. *Ibid.*, Art. 1869.
671. *Ibid.*
672. *Ibid.*, Art. 1874.
673. *Ibid.*, Art. 1881.
674. *Ibid.*, Art. 1887.
675. *Ibid.*, Art. 1910.
676. *Ibid.*
677. *Ibid.*
678. *Ibid.*, Art. 1911. *See also Professional Services, Inc. v. Court of Appeals*, 544 SCRA 170 (2008).
679. *Ibid.*, Art. 1884.
680. *Ibid.*

client.[681] And in terms of accountability and the custody of money, agents must also render an account of all transactions of the client and give or return to the client whatever the agent might have received by virtue of the agency, regardless of the client's ownership.[682]

361. The sports agent-athlete relationship is characterized as a fiduciary relationship, with the agent owing the client a duty of loyalty.[683] Hence, agents who find themselves in a conflict of interest situation must, in all cases, choose the interest of the client before their own, lest they be liable to their client.[684] Lawyers who also assume the role of agents have another level of compliance when it comes to conflict situations; under the Code of Professional Responsibility, lawyers should not represent conflicting interests and open themselves up to administrative sanctions when they do.[685]

362. A contract of agency is generally revocable at will because it is mainly based on the principal's trust and confidence in his or her agent.[686] A sports agent may withdraw from the agency by notifying the client-athlete.[687] However, even after withdrawing, the agent must still act as such until he or she has had a reasonable opportunity to take the necessary steps to meet the situation.[688] If the principal suffers any damage because of the withdrawal, the agent must indemnify the principal for it.[689]

363. On the side of the client-athlete, revocation of agency by the client-athlete will not prejudice third persons who act in good faith and without knowledge of the revocation,[690] mainly because the said revocation is an intramural matter between the agent and the client-athlete. The law mandates the notice of revocation to be done in broadsheets to bind third parties,[691] but if the agent had been previously dealing with specific third parties, due notice must be given to these specific parties.[692]

681. *Ibid.*, Art. 1888.
682. *Ibid.*, Art. 1891.
683. *Detroit Lions, Inc. v. Argovitz*, 580 F. Supp. 542 (E.D. Mich. 1984).
684. *Ibid.*, Art. 1889.
685. Code of Professional Responsibility, Rule 15.03 (1988).
686. *Republic v. Evangelista*, 466 SCRA 544, 551 (2005).
687. Civil Code of the Philippines, Art. 1927.
688. *Ibid.*, Art. 1929.
689. *Ibid.*
690. *Ibid.*, Art. 1922.
691. *Ibid.*
692. *Ibid.*, Art. 1921.

§4. DATA PRIVACY

364. The Data Privacy Act of 2012 (DPA) and its IRR have greatly impacted how sports businesses have been conducted.[693] Teams, retailers, and even universities have had to comply with the provisions of the DPA and its IRR, lest they face stiff penalties and fines.

365. Compliance in the sports sector might not be explicit in the DPA, but sports teams and businesses are undoubtedly covered by the DPA and its IRR. The DPA and its IRR apply to any natural or juridical persons involved in the processing of personal data in the Philippines or of personal data about a Philippine citizen or resident.[694] It also covers entities that have branches, agencies, offices, or subsidiaries in the Philippines where the parent or foreign affiliate has access to personal data.[695]

366. It covers both personal information controllers (PIC) and personal information processors (PIP). A PIC is a natural or juridical person who controls the processing of personal data or instructs another to process personal data on its behalf.[696] A PIP is anyone to whom a PIC may outsource or instruct the processing of personal data.[697] As a PIC may outsource the processing of personal data, the PIC must use contractual or other reasonable means to ensure the PIP complies with the DPA and its IRR.[698]

367. "Processing" refers to any operation performed on personal data.[699] This includes the collection and recording of data, whether through automated means or manual processing, such as a filing system.[700] A sports team, for example, is covered by the DPA, as it controls and collects personal data of its employees, coaching, staff, and players.

368. As such, teams must comply with obligations imposed by the DPA and its IRR. The first obligation revolves around the DPA principles. It must ensure that the processing of personal data should adhere to the DPA principles of transparency, legitimate purpose, and proportionality.[701]

369. Transparency means that the data subject must be aware of the nature, purpose, and extent of the processing of his or her personal data.[702] Hence, sports teams

693. *See* Data Privacy Act of 2012, Republic Act No. 10173 (2012); Implementing Rules and Regulations ("IRR") of the Data Privacy Act of 2012 (NPC, Aug. 4, 2016).
694. IRR of the Data Privacy Act of 2012, §4.
695. *Ibid.*
696. IRR of the Data Privacy Act of 2012, §3(m).
697. *Ibid.*, §3(n).
698. *Ibid.*, §43.
699. *Ibid.*, §n 3(o).
700. *Ibid.*
701. *Ibid.*, §18.
702. *Ibid.*

and businesses must use clear and plain language in communicating with their data subjects (such as their employees, players, and even fans) information regarding their data processing.

370. Legitimate purpose means that the processing of information shall be compatible with a declared and specific purpose.[703] For example, a sports arena owner's purpose for data collection must be legitimate and must be communicated to its patrons.

371. Proportionality means that the processing of information shall be adequate, suitable, and necessary in relation to the declared and specific purpose.[704] Hence, sports teams should only collect and process data necessary for their operations. It should not collect more data than necessary. This is an important factor for teams building marketing databases of their fans.

372. The IRR provides criteria to determine whether the processing of personal data is lawful.[705] One criterion is that the data subject must have given his consent prior to the collection or as soon as practicable and reasonable.[706] Consent is required prior to the collection and processing of personal data, subject to certain exemptions provided by the DPA and other laws.[707] The IRR allows a PIC to process personal data even when a data subject objects or withholds consent when it is necessary or desirable in the context of an employer-employee relationship.[708] Hence, there may be some information that may be required by employer-teams from their employee-players, even if the disclosure of said data is objected to by the employee-player.

---

703. *Ibid.*

704. *Ibid.*

705. *Ibid.*, §21.

706. *Ibid.*, §21 The rest of the criteria are as follows:

(a) the data subject must have given his or her consent prior to the collection, or as soon as practicable and reasonable;
(b) the processing involves the personal information of a data subject who is a party to a contractual agreement, in order to fulfill obligations under the contract or to take steps at the request of the data subject prior to entering the said agreement;
(c) the processing is necessary for compliance with a legal obligation to which the personal information controller is subject;
(d) the processing is necessary to protect vitally important interests of the data subject, including his or her life and health;
(e) the processing of personal information is necessary to respond to national emergency or to comply with the requirements of public order and safety, as prescribed by law;
(f) the processing of personal information is necessary for the fulfillment of the constitutional or statutory mandate of a public authority; or
(g) the processing is necessary to pursue the legitimate interests of the personal information controller, or by a third party or parties to whom the data is disclosed, except where such interests are overridden by fundamental rights and freedoms of the data subject, which require protection under the Philippine Constitution.

707. *Ibid.*, §19(a)(1).

708. *Ibid.*, §34(b)(2).

373. The DPA, however, exempts certain kinds of information from being processed. These are classified as sensitive, personal and privileged information.[709] Sensitive information includes a person's race, ethnic origin, marital status, age, religious, or political affiliations; a person's health, education, genetic, or sexual life; any proceeding for any offense committed or alleged to have been committed by the person (including the disposition of such cases); and information issued by government agencies peculiar to persons, such as social security numbers, tax returns, and licenses.[710]

374. Sensitive information may only be processed under certain conditions, such as when consent is given by the data subject, prior to the processing of sensitive personal information.[711] Hence, teams must obtain the consent of their players before it collects and processes these types of information. This extra step of consent should not be taken for granted, as unauthorized processing of sensitive information is a crime punishable by imprisonment and a fine.[712]

375. The second general obligation involves data sharing. Sports businesses must ensure that before it shares personal data with third persons, it must get the data subject's consent for data sharing.[713] Consent is required even when the data is to be shared with an affiliate or mother company.[714] The data subject should be provided with certain information (such as the identity of the entity who will be given access to the personal data and the purpose of the sharing, among others) before collection or before the data is shared.[715] This is particularly relevant to school transfers of student-athletes and trades of professional athletes.

376. The third general obligation focuses on structural measures to ensure data protection. The PIC and PIP should implement reasonable organizational, physical, and technical security measures to protect personal data.

377. In terms of organizational security measures, the PIC and PIP should designate an individual as data protection officer (DPO) who shall be accountable for ensuring compliance with the DPA and its IRR. For entities which have branches and suboffices, a compliance officer for privacy (COP) may also be appointed for each component unit.[716] One of the duties of the DPO or COP is to ensure the conduct of privacy impact assessments on the data processes of the PIC or PIP and ensure proper procedures are followed if or when there is a data breach or security incident regarding the PIC or PIP's data.[717]

709. *Ibid.*, §22.
710. *Ibid.*, §3(t).
711. *Ibid.*, §22.
712. *Ibid.*, §52.
713. *Ibid.*, §20.
714. *Ibid.*, §20(b)(1).
715. *Ibid.*, §20(b)(3).
716. Designation of Data Protection Officers, NPC Advisory No. 2017-01 (NPC, Mar. 14, 2017) (hereinafter "NPC Advisory").
717. *Ibid.*

378. The DPO should be a full-time or organic employee of the PIC and PIP.[718] The DPO should have expertise in relevant privacy or data protection policies and practices and also be familiar with the operations being carried out by the PIC or the PIP.[719] The DPO or COP should be a regular or permanent position; if the employment of the DPO or COP is based on a contract, the term or duration thereof should at least be two years to ensure stability.[720]

379. The PIC or PIP should also implement data protection policies that provide for the organization, physical, and technical security measures.[721] It must also maintain records that sufficiently describe its data processing system and identify the duties and responsibilities of those individuals who have access to personal data. These include those who work in a team's or company's human resources (HR) department.[722] It must also ensure that its HR department complies with the DPA and its IRR. In terms of physical security measures, the PIC or PIP must ensure that its office space and workstations are arranged to provide privacy for anyone processing personal data.[723] In terms of technical security measures, the PIC or PIP must adopt policies to protect personal data and safeguards to protect their computer networks against breaches that might affect data integrity and confidentiality.[724]

380. In sum, teams, sports businesses, and universities with sports programs must designate a DPO, draft and implement its data privacy policy that covers the protection of its data and its computer systems, maintain records of its data processing system, and ensure that its workstations are adequate to provide privacy.

381. A bare minimum obligation is the protection of the rights of the data subjects. These rights include the following: the right to be informed, which includes, but is not limited to, the right of the data subject to know the scope and method of the data processing, the purpose behind the processing, and the existence of these rights;[725] the right to object to the processing of personal data and to withhold content, except in instances where consent is not necessary (such as when the collection and processing are needed in the context of an employer-employee relationship);[726] the right to access the data;[727] the right to rectify errors in data;[728] and the right to remove the data from the PIC's system, under certain conditions.[729]

---

718. *Ibid.*
719. *Ibid.*
720. *Ibid.*
721. IRR of the Data Privacy Act of 2012, 26 (b).
722. *Ibid.*, §26(c).
723. *Ibid.*, §27(b).
724. *Ibid.*, §28.
725. *Ibid.*, §34(a).
726. *Ibid.*, §34(b).
727. *Ibid.*, §34(c).
728. *Ibid.*, §34(d).
729. *Ibid.*, §34(e).

382. Aside from these substantial obligations, there are also monitoring and reportorial obligations imposed by the DPA for data breaches. In the event of a data breach or reasonable belief that a data breach has occurred, the DPO must notify the NPC and the affected data subjects of the breach within seventy-two hours.[730] Failure to do so is a crime punishable by imprisonment and a fine.[731]

383. Finally, the PIC or the PIP must register its personal data processing system with the NPC, if it employs 250 or more persons, the processing it carries out is likely to pose a risk to the rights and freedoms of data subjects; the processing is not occasional (more than once a year); or the processing includes sensitive personal information of at least 1,000 individuals.[732]

§5. Intellectual Property

I. Trademarks

384. The Intellectual Property Code (IPC) of the Philippines is the governing law for anything related to intellectual property in the Philippines. Patterned after the Lanham Act of the U.S., the IPC mirrors this Act, and the statutory construction principle of "adopted statutes" should apply.[733] The government agency tasked to implement the IPC is the Intellectual Property Office (IPO).

385. Trademarks are particularly relevant to Philippine sports law, especially as athletes and businesses use trademarks to build their brands and monetize their popularity. Under the IPC, a trademark is a sign that distinguishes one's goods and services from another.[734] Registration with the IPO, however, is essential for the protection of trademarks as trademark owners only get the rights in a mark through registration.[735] Generally, only when a trademark is registered will it be given protection by the law.[736] Once registered, third parties may not use it without the owner's consent.[737] Registration lasts for ten years and may be renewed for periods of ten years.[738]

---

730. *Ibid.*, §38.
731. *Ibid.*, §57.
732. *Ibid.*, §47.
733. *Sanchez v. Hon. Hernando and Pacquiao*, C.A.-G.R. SP No. 104070, 2 (Court of Appeals Special 17th Division, 2009) *cited in* Lolibeth R. Medrano & John Paulo Vicencio, *Under the Shadows of Trademark: The Current State of Publicity Rights in the Philippines,* 63 Ateneo L.J. 689 (2019).
734. Intellectual Property Code of the Philippines, Republic Act. No. 8293, *amended by* Republic Act Nos. 9150, 9502, and 10372, §121.1.
735. *Ibid.*, §122.
736. An unregistered trademark can still be protected if one is able to prove that one has been using the mark even before registration. *See E.Y. Industrial Sales, Inc. v. Shen Dar Electricity and Machinery Co., Ltd.*, 634 SCRA 363 (2010).
737. Intellectual Property Code of the Philippines, §121.
738. *Ibid.*, §§145 and 146.

386. Not all logos or marks can be registered. The IPO will disallow marks which are immoral, deceptive, or scandalous,[739] disparages or falsely suggests a connection with a person (whether living or dead), institutions, beliefs, or national symbols;[740]may bring contempt or disrepute to another,[741] has the Philippine flag (or flag of another country) on it,[742] includes the name, portrait, or signature of a living person, except with his consent,[743] uses the portrait of a dead President, during the life of his/her spouse, except with the latter's consent;[744] are misleading as to nature, quality, characteristic, or geographical origin,[745] are generic or simply identify the product they will be used on,[746] are simply descriptive of the product,[747] or are contrary to public order or morals.[748]

387. Maintaining registered trademarks requires the filing of certain documents with the IPO. The IPO requires the filing of a Declaration of Actual Use certificate and proof of use of the trademark within three years from the filing of the application, one year from the fifth anniversary of the date of its registration, within one year from renewal, and within one year from the fifth anniversary of each renewal.[749] Proof of use can be made by showing photographs of goods with the trademark attached to them and even brochures or advertising materials showing the actual use of the trademark.[750]

388. Trademark owners who enter into licensing agreements with licensees must register said agreements with the IPO. Under the IPC, unregistered licensing agreements do not bind and have no effect against third parties.[751] An increasing number of sports licensing agreements have been entered into by rightsholders in recent years. Because of the growing popularity of collegiate sports, both the athletic associations and their respective schools have licensed their trademarks to different clothing brands and merchandise. Recently, the UAAP entered into a licensing agreement with the global sports brand, New Era, a testament to the marketing power of collegiate sports.[752] There have been issues involving the extent that an athletic association can license trademarks owned by a member school, but these have been resolved amicably and through contract interpretation.

---

739. *Ibid.*, §123.1(a).
740. *Ibid.*
741. *Ibid.*
742. *Ibid.*, §123.1(b).
743. *Ibid.*, §123.1(c).
744. *Ibid.*, §123.1(c).
745. *Ibid.*, §123.1(g).
746. *Ibid.*, §123.1(h).
747. *Ibid.*, §123.1(j).
748. *Ibid.*, §123.1(m).
749. Trademark Regulations of 2017, Memorandum Circular No. 17-010, Rule 204 (IPOPHL, Jul. 7, 2017).
750. *Ibid.*, Rule 210.
751. Intellectual Property Code of the Philippines, §150.
752. Anton Roxas, *SWAG ON: The UAAP Gears Up with New Era PH*, ABS-CBN (Jul. 29, 2018), https://sports.abs-cbn.com/uaap/news/2018/07/29/swag-on-the-uaap-gears-new-era-ph-45066.

II. Right of Publicity

389. In a nutshell, the right of publicity is a person's right to commercially exploit their name, image, or likeness. While this right has been recognized in common law or in statute in the United States, the right of publicity has yet to find its way into Philippine jurisprudence or in express provisions of law.[753] This, of course, does not mean that said right is not recognized in the Philippines.[754]

390. Athletes or rightsholders who find their right of publicity abused or misused by third parties have section 169.1(a) of the IPC to hinge their claims. Section 169.1 refers to False Designations of Origin or False Description or Representation, and states as follows:

> SECTION 169. *False Designations of Origin; False Description or Representation.*—169.1. Any person who, on or in connection with any goods or services, or any container for goods, uses in commerce any word, term, name, symbol, or device, or any combination thereof, or any false designation of origin, false or misleading description of fact, or false or misleading representation of fact, which:
>
> (a) Is likely to cause confusion, or to cause mistake, or to deceive as to the affiliation, connection, or association of such person with another person, or as to the origin, sponsorship, or approval of his or her goods, services, or commercial activities by another person.[755]

Anyone found guilty of false designation is looking at a criminal offense with penalties of imprisonment from two to five years and a fine from PDP 50,000 to PDP 200,000.[756]

391. One such athlete who has used section 169.1 to protect his right of publicity is none other than Manny Pacquiao. In a 2009 case, the Court of Appeals recognized the boxer's right of publicity when he sued G2K Corporation (G2K) and In-A-Jiffy Enterprises (IAJ), the purveyors of the popular videoke product "Wow Magic Sing Microphone," a staple of almost every Filipino party and get-together.[757] As Pacquiao has been known for dabbling in multiplying disciplines, it was only fitting that Pacquiao's battle with G2K and IAJ stemmed not from boxing career but his musical career. As an aside, the boxer loved to sing, a passion he

753. Medrano & Vicencio, *supra* note 733, at 755.
754. *Ibid.*
755. Intellectual Property Code of the Philippines, §169.1.
756. *Ibid.*, §170.
757. *Sanchez,* C.A. G.R. SP No. 104070 at 2.

leveraged with his popularity to record multiple musical albums—a song of which he used when he walked to the ring in his fight against Floyd Mayweather in 2015.[758]

392. The issue arose when G2K and IAJ purchased copies of Pacquiao's latest album and gave these out for free for every purchase of the "Wow Magic Sing."[759] Pacquiao then proceeded to sue G2K and IAJ for misrepresentation and unlawfully using his name, image, and goodwill without his consent.[760] G2K and IAJ filed a motion to quash, which the trial court denied, stating Pacquiao's rights were protected under section 169.1.[761]

393. In its appeal, G2K and IAJ claimed that prior trademark registration was required before Pacquiao's image could be protected under the IPC. The Court of Appeals rejected such argument claiming that Pacquiao's high-profile status and name should be protected from unauthorized endorsements under section 169.1.[762] The decision suggests that trademark registration is not a prerequisite for protection against unauthorized product endorsements.[763] While the Court of Appeals decisions do not form part of Philippine jurisprudence, these decisions are highly persuasive.[764]

394. In any case, the decision makes logical sense, given the explicit wording of section 169.1. With that said, finding a basis for the right of publicity in the law of trademarks also makes sense from a policy perspective. The fact that the law of trademarks operates to protect the goodwill of brands also applies to high-profile athletes who themselves are living and walking "brands."[765] The public and rightsholders should be protected from the confusion and danger of unauthorized designations and representations either way, whether the mark or brand is registered in the traditional sense or a living person.

395. The ideal, of course, would either have the Supreme Court explicitly recognize the right of publicity in a decision or have Congress amend the IPC to make it a statutory right. Until then, section 169.1, along with Manny Pacquiao's off-ring victory, is the next best thing.

758. Dan Carson, *Manny Pacquiao Ring Walk: Philippines Star to Walk Out to His Own Song,* Bleach Report (May 3, 2015), https://bleacherreport.com/articles/2450147-manny-pacquiao-ring-walk-philippines-star-to-walk-out-to-his-own-song.
759. *Sanchez,* C.A. G.R. SP No. 104070 at 3.
760. *Ibid.,* at 4.
761. *Ibid.,* at 9.
762. *Ibid.,* at 11.
763. Medrano & Vicencio, *supra* note 733, at 766.
764. *United Coconut Planters Bank v. Uy,* 850 SCRA 298, 307 (2018).
765. Medrano & Vicencio, *supra* note 733, at 774.

Part V. COVID-19 and Its Impact on National Sport

Chapter 1. Background and Government Measures

396. When COVID-19 struck in early 2020, it sent the sports world reeling. The Philippines was no exception. In the early stages of the pandemic, sports events were simply postponed. However, when the reality struck that the pandemic was going to overstay its welcome, these events started to be canceled one by one.

397. Amateur and collegiate sports were the first to feel the brunt of COVID-19—with schools closed or moved to online learning, collegiate leagues such as the UAAP had to cancel their season midway.[766] The NCAA also ended abruptly.[767]

398. Professional sports soon followed suit. The PBA was suspended indefinitely one game into its 2020 season.[768] The PFL was also forced to postpone its 2020 season.[769] Fortunately, the PBA and the PFL managed to pull off "bubble seasons" in the last quarter of 2020. This, however, could not be said of the PVL; its season was canceled in May 2020 and is looking to resume only in 2021.[770] The PVL's rival women's volleyball league, the PSL, was not so lucky, with COVID-19-related issues essentially forcing its teams to join the PVL and marking the end of the PSL.

399. COVID-19 also took a toll on the country's national and international sports events. The ASEAN Para Games was canceled due to budgetary concerns

766. David Tristan Yumol, *UAAP Board Cancels Season 82 due to COVID-19 Pandemic*, CNN Philippines (Apr. 17, 2020), https://cnnphilippines.com/sports/2020/4/7/uaap-cancels-season-82-covid-pandemic.html.
767. Ivan Stewart Saldajeno, *NCAA Season 95 Ended due to Covid-19*, Philippine News Agency (Mar. 19, 2020), https://www.pna.gov.ph/articles/1097211.
768. Ma. Angelica Garcia, *PBA Suspends Games Indefinitely due to COVID-19 Threat*, GMA News Online (Mar. 11, 2020), https://www.gmanetwork.com/news/sports/basketball/729223/pba-suspends-games-indefinitely-due-to-covid-19/story/.
769. ABS-CBN News Staff, *PFF Still Awaiting IATF Go-Signal for Football's Return*, ABS-CBN News (Jun. 29, 2020), https://news.abs-cbn.com/sports/06/29/20/pff-still-awaiting-iatf-go-signal-for-footballs-return.
770. Ohmer Bautista, *PVL to Start 2020 Season with Open Conference, Mulls Opening Day Reset*, Tiebreaker Times (Apr. 19, 2020), https://tiebreakertimes.com.ph/tbt/pvl-start-2020-season-open-conference-mulls-opening-day-reset/183611.

brought on by the pandemic.[771] The Palarong Pambansa, a nationwide government-sponsored athletics and sports meet for children, was also canceled.[772]

400. These cancelations were not simply initiated out of an abundance of caution by its organizers. These cancelations were, in fact, government mandated. The PSC was one of the first government authorities to issue a COVID-19-related mandate specific to sports, when it released a March 12, 2020 directive that restricted travel for national athletes and required a fourteen-day quarantine for athletes returning from abroad.[773] This was pursuant to Presidential Proclamation No. 922 which declared a state of public health emergency throughout the Philippines.

401. On March 16, 2020, President Duterte placed the entire Luzon island on an enhanced community quarantine (ECQ) which effectively put all sports on hold, as most professional leagues are based in Metro Manila. The following day, the President signed Presidential Proclamation No. 929 which changed the previous declaration of a state of public health emergency into a state of calamity over the entire country. As an indication of how the government has handled the pandemic, the President issued Presidential Proclamation No. 1021 on September 16, 2020, which extended the state of calamity all the way to September 21, 2021.

402. While Congress would pass various laws with the hope to boost the economy and improve the plight brought about by COVID-19, these laws did not have as much impact on sports as President Duterte's community quarantine classifications which he puzzlingly would announce past midnight in taped press conferences. These quarantine classifications were confusing both as to their terminology—modified general community quarantine, general community quarantine, modified enhanced community quarantine, ECQ—and as to their specific rules for travel, work, curfew, and public transportation. In any case, these classifications would also outline rules on sports and mass gatherings, so anyone who sought to engage in any kind of athletic activity had to reckon with the community quarantine rules covering a specific location in the Philippines.

403. Given the responsibility of overseeing the pandemic response was the Inter-Agency Task Force on Emerging Infectious Diseases (IATF). The IATF—along with the GAB, the DOH, and the PSC—would be vital in the return of sports, as organizers were required to get approval from the government before any sports events were to be conducted.

---

771. Moch. Fiqih Prawira Adjie, *2020 ASEAN Para Games Official Canceled*, The Jakarta Post (May 9, 2020), https://www.thejakartapost.com/news/2020/05/09/2020-asean-para-games-officially-canceled.html.

772. ABS-CBN News Staff, *PSC Cancels Sports Events, Assures Support for National Athletes*, ABS-CBN News (Apr. 29, 2020), https://news.abs-cbn.com/sports/04/29/20/psc-cancels-sports-events-assures-support-for-national-athletes.

773. Philippine Sports Commission, *Policy Directives of the Philippine Sports Commission on COVID-19*, (Mar. 12, 2020), https://www.facebook.com/PhlSportsCommission/posts/policy-directives-ofphilippine-sports-commission-on-covid-19pursuant-to-presiden/2983875238302430/ (last visited May 26, 2021).

Chapter 2. Fortuitous or Not?

404. The sudden shutdown of sports was disruptive, to say the least, particularly to sports contracts. The same could be said for the underlying contracts that supported sports events, such as sponsorship contracts, lease contracts between the organizer and the venue-owner, licensing agreements between rightsholders and media companies, contracts between the ticketholders and organizers, even security service contracts between a venue-owner and a security agency. With sports at a virtual standstill in the early stages of the pandemic, one of the first questions in everyone's minds was "what do we with our contracts?"

405. Article 1174 of the Civil Code of the Philippines quickly came to mind. The provision talks about fortuitous events and their impact on existing contracts. It states, "Except in cases expressly specified by the law, or when it is otherwise declared by stipulation, or when the nature of the obligation requires the assumption of risk, no person shall be responsible for those events which could not be foreseen, or which though foreseen, were inevitable."[774]

406. Simply put, no one can be held liable for the non-performance of a contractual obligation if the reason therefor was a fortuitous event. This, of course, begged the question, "is COVID-19 a fortuitous event?"

407. While there is no definitive answer yet (given the turtle-like pace that cases take to the Supreme Court), jurisprudence provides four essential requisites for an event to be considered fortuitous: first, the cause of the breach of the obligation must be independent of the will of the debtor; second, the event must be either unforeseeable or unavoidable; third, the event must be such as to render it impossible for the debtor to fulfill his obligation in a normal manner; and fourth, the debtor must be free from any participation in or aggravation of the injury to the creditor.[775]

408. Applying all four elements, it seems COVID-19 can be considered a fortuitous event that would excuse performance of obligations.[776]

409. First, the cause of the canceled contracts or breached obligations was independent of the will of the debtor, who may be the organizer or rightsholder.[777] It would also be ludicrous to blame the birth of the virus on anyone, let alone a sports organizer in the Philippines.

---

774. Civil Code of the Philippines, Art. 1174.
775. *Nakpil v. Court of Appeals*, 144 SCRA 597 (1986).
776. Mickey Ingles, *Covid-19: Fortuitous Event or Not?*, Batas Sportiva (Mar. 10, 2020), https://batassportiva.com/2020/03/10/covid-19-fortuitous-event-or-not/.
777. *Ibid.*

410. Second, the spread of COVID-19 in the country was unforeseeable or unavoidable.[778] Parties could not have predicted that a pandemic would strike like a plague of biblical proportions when they entered into the affected contracts before COVID-19 reared its ugly head.

411. Third, the pervasiveness of COVID-19 had made it impossible for organizers to fulfill their legal duty to ensure the health and safety of both the participants and spectators of canceled events.[779] At the early stages of the pandemic, protocols had yet to exist that would allow the return of sports in a healthy and safe fashion. Add the fact that the government itself prohibited sports, and it becomes clear that sports-related obligations would have been impossible to fulfill.

412. Finally, parties presumably did not participate in or aggravate any injuries sustained by their contractual counterparts.[780] On the flip side, the cancelations actually helped stop the spread of the disease by limiting exposure to the virus.[781]

413. It seems COVID-19 could be considered a fortuitous event. And barring the three exceptions in Article 1174 when a debtor may still be held despite a fortuitous event, there should be no liability for cancelations because of COVID-19.

414. It remains difficult to determine how actual contracts were affected and how contractual disputes arising from COVID-19 were resolved. Whether these were brought to court or settled out of court, it is nearly impossible to put a number on it. One thing is certain: succeeding contracts have taken into account possible contingencies for future fortuitous events.

---

778. *Ibid.*
779. *Ibid.*
780. *Ibid.*
781. *Ibid.*

Chapter 3. Resumption of Sports

415. In late July 2020, the GAB, the DOH, and the PSC issued a joint administrative order (JAO) that effectively allowed professional sports to return under strict conditions.[782] With different leagues considering sports bubbles similar to those organized in the US, questions soon emerged regarding the legal issues surrounding sports bubbles.

416. The first bubble to get into trouble involved the collegiate basketball team of the University of Santo Tomas (UST), which held a training bubble in the province of Sorsogon.[783] Some players went on social media to complain about their food and living conditions.[784] Understandably, the public was shocked and outraged by the players' revelation, especially since only *professional* teams were allowed to resume sports and that classes had shifted to purely online learning. Why the coaching staff pushed through with training that involved shuttling the student-athletes across different provinces *despite* the pandemic was anyone's guess. The UAAP issued an indefinite ban on head coach Aldin Ayo, who not only had his players train but also had them attend farming seminars and visit a piggery.[785] The exodus of the team's stars immediately followed the controversy.[786] Soon after, the IATF, the Department of Justice, and the CHED stepped in with their respective probes.[787]

417. Given the heat generated by the burst UST bubble, it was only right that leagues who wished to start their own bubbles err on the side of caution. Writing for Rappler.com, the author provided five legal considerations that sports bubble organizers have to take note of.[788]

418. First, the most basic legal consideration is to comply with government directives[789]—something that the UST bubble was seemingly guilty of violating. These government directives come in the form of IATF Guidelines which are then approved by the President.[790] Hence, the site of proposed bubbles must first consider the quarantine level of the locality, as these would then affect the rules on public gatherings. Quarantine levels also affect whether players and coaches of a certain age can participate, as general IATF Guidelines require those below 21 and over 60 to stay home.[791]

---

782. ABS-CBN News Staff, *"Wait Is Over" for PBA, PFF as Order Signed for Practices to Resume*, ABS-CBN News (Jul. 27, 2020), https://news.abs-cbn.com/sports/07/27/20/wait-is-over-for-pba-pff-as-order-signed-for-practices-to-resume.
783. Delfin Dioquino, *TIMELINE: Chaos Follows as UST Bubble Bursts*, Rappler (Sept. 10, 2020), https://www.rappler.com/sports/uaap/timeline-chaos-follows-ust-bubble.
784. *Ibid.*
785. *Ibid.*
786. *Ibid.*
787. *Ibid.*
788. Mickey Ingles, *Exploring 5 Legal Considerations of Sports Bubbles*, Rappler (Sep. 15, 2020), https://www.rappler.com/sports/exploring-five-legal-considerations-of-sports-bubbles.
789. *Ibid.*
790. *Ibid.*
791. *Ibid.*

419. Second, coordination and approval from the relevant government agencies are essential.[792] Professional leagues have to comply with the JAO.[793] University- and college-based teams must comply with CHED Guidelines before resuming sports activity. As of May 2021, no university- and college-based sports have resumed in Metro Manila.

420. Third, bubble organizers must comply with their duty to anticipate foreseeable dangers.[794] Under Philippine tort law, organizers have the basic legal duty to anticipate and prevent reasonably foreseeable dangers. The spread of COVID-19 is arguably a foreseeable danger that must be prevented. As a standard, government guidelines will be the minimum benchmark for determining whether an organizer has complied with or breached its legal duty.

421. For schools, the CHED Guidelines will be the minimum requirement for school training bubbles.[795] However, schools must still exhibit a higher diligence in creating their bubbles—especially if some student-athletes are minors or below 18 years old because schools, their administrators, and teachers have special parental authority and responsibility over minor children under their supervision, instruction, or custody in all authorized activities, whether inside or outside the school premises.[796]

422. Regardless of how sports resume (whether these be in a bubble or a closed-circuit arrangement), the organizers must also ensure basic bubble protocol, which will be part of their applications for approval with the IATF. Given the length of the pandemic, these basic protocols—access to testing, masks, shields, and healthcare professionals—have been taken for granted, but these must still be complied with.[797] With vaccines slowly being rolled out in the Philippines as of May 2020, access to vaccines must also be considered by organizers as part of basic bubble protocol.

423. Fourth, organizers must engage their stakeholders, particularly the players and coaches, in ironing out the details of the bubble.[798] Players should be allowed to opt-out of the bubble for valid health reasons.[799] The legal effects of opting out have to be ironed out in negotiations with the stakeholders, particularly when it comes to the salary of those opting out.[800] In the same light, student-athletes who

792. *Ibid.*
793. *Ibid.*
794. *Ibid.*
795. *Ibid.*
796. The Family Code of the Philippines, Executive Order No. 209, Art. 218 (1987).
797. Ingles, *supra* note 788.
798. *Ibid.*
799. *Ibid.*
800. *Ibid.*

opt out must also be given a chance to be heard on whether their opt-out year will be counted as a playing year for eligibility purposes and how it will affect their athletic scholarships.[801]

424. Finally, bubble organizers must disclose as much as possible and adopt a policy of openness.[802] Learning from the successful NBA bubble and the unsuccessful UST bubble, the benefits of openness far outweigh the potential disadvantages of public scrutiny. A policy of transparency not only gives the bubble a sense of legality and legitimacy but also actually helps with fan engagement.[803] The curious nature of bubbles helps give them the veneer of a reality show, with the sports-deprived public eager to gobble up any content from players and journalists within the bubble.

425. With that said, the PBA, PFL, and 3×3 finally hosted their own bubbles with varying levels of success in the last quarter of 2020. As of May 2022, these three leagues have successfully organized non-bubble seasons, taking into consideration limited seating capacities in stadia.[804]

426. However, other leagues outside the Metro Manila area have taken advantage of the more lenient community quarantines in the provinces and resumed tournaments. For example, the Chooks To Go Pilipinas VisMin Cup, a basketball league in the Visayas and Mindanao regions of the country, resumed the Visayas leg of its tournament in mid-April, only for it to be marred by a strange game that reeked of match-fixing.[805] The PSL also held a beach volleyball tournament in Subic in March 2021.[806] As expected, professional eSports was quick to adjust to the challenges of the pandemic. The ever-popular Mobile Legends Professional League—Philippines capped off its seventh Season in October 2020 and began its eighth Season in March 2021.

427. Unfortunately, the pandemic did not deter poorly managed professional teams from taking advantage of players. In mid-2020, PFL team Global FC was put in hot water after social media posts of players alleged that Global FC had completely reneged in their payments.[807] The players—recruited from abroad, signed,

801. *Ibid.*
802. *Ibid.*
803. *Ibid.*
804. CNN Staff, *PBA Allows Full Capacity Crowd Amid Alert Level 1 Shift*, CNN Philippines (Mar. 1, 2022), https://www.cnnphilippines.com/sports/2022/3/1/PBA-full-audience-capacity-Alert-Level-1.html.
805. Delfin Dioquino, *GAB Chief Warns VisMin Super Cup, Probes Controversial Game*, Rappler (Apr. 14, 2021), https://www.rappler.com/sports/gab-chief-warns-vismin-super-cup-probes-controversial-game.
806. Niel Victor C. Masoy, *Abanse Negrense a Rules 2021 PSL Beach Volley*, The Manila Times (Mar. 1, 2021), https://www.manilatimes.net/2021/03/01/sports/sports-top/abanse-negrense-a-rules-2021-psl-beach-volley/846192/.
807. Beatrice Go, *Unpaid Global FC Players Can Seek PH Football Federation's Assistance*, Rappler (Aug. 5, 2020), https://www.rappler.com/sports/football/unpaid-global-fc-players-seek-assistance-philippine-football-league-federation.

and promised plane tickets to the Philippines—were left with nothing but excuses from the team's management.[808] Aggrieved Japanese player Ryo Fujii subsequently filed a case in front of the FIFA Dispute Resolution Chamber and was awarded GBP 26,500 for Global FC's failure to comply with its obligations.[809] Until today, Global FC has yet to pay Ryo Fujii and has subsequently been banned from registering new players at both the local and international levels.[810]

428. If there was any silver lining in the dark clouds brought by the pandemic, it was Joint Resolution No. 2020-01 issued by GAB and the PSC on October 16, 2020. The Resolution finally defined the meaning of "professional athlete" and "professional sports or competitions" in the Philippine setting. While these two phrases would seem too simple to even define, the non-delineation of professional sports and amateur sports brought avoidable issues—one of which was whether or not an athlete or a competition needed a license from GAB, the government agency tasked to regulate professional sports.

429. Under the Joint Resolution, "professional athletes" referred to any athlete who is paid a sum of money for participating in a sport, excluding, however, any token amounts for uniforms, lodging, transportation, and other training expenses.[811] "Professional sports or competitions," in a nutshell, referred to sports where professional athletes participated or competed in *or* those that are conducted for profit.[812]

430. The Joint Resolution was essential in the resumption of sports. As only professional sports were allowed to resume, leagues which were operating professionally in everything but name (such as the PVL and the PSL) were forced to rethink their "non-professional" status just to resume sports and stem the financial losses of canceled seasons. These leagues had to either finally admit that they were professional and register with the GAB or stay amateur and not get the green light to play.

431. The PVL took the plunge and "went pro" by applying for a GAB license in November 2020.[813] Again, the author uses quotation marks to qualify the phrase "went pro," as the PVL's teams had been paying their players quite handsomely and definitely more than the token amounts alluded to in the Joint Resolution. Its rival league, the PSL, did not. What followed was an exodus of PSL teams and players

---

808. *Ibid.*
809. FIFA DRC, *Employment-Related Dispute Concerning the Player Ryo Fujii (Ryo Fujii, Japan v. Global FC, Philippines)*, Decision of the DRC Judge, Ref. No. 20-01436 (Dec. 9, 2020).
810. FIFA E-mail to author, Apr. 13, 2021.
811. Games and Amusements Board & Philippine Sports Commission, *Guidelines on the Definitions of Professional Athlete and Professional Sports or Competitions*, Joint Resolution No. 2020-01, https://gab.gov.ph/wp-content/uploads/2020/10/GAB-AND-PSC-JOINT-RESOLUTION-1.pdf?fbclid=IwAR02h7yH7gFUfbM6tQcCmM0f_N5aLVorKjWxTNc_5rMMKBTONqMaP2ibHYA (last visited May 27, 2021).
812. *Ibid.*
813. Lance Agcaoili, *PVL Team Owners Agree Pro Status Will Take League to New Heights*, Spin.ph (Nov. 14, 2020), https://www.spin.ph/volleyball/pvl/pvl-team-owners-agree-pro-status-will-take-league-to-new-heights-a2522-20201114.

moving to the PVL.[814] With the GAB license in hand, the PVL had something the PSL did not—a chance to hold a tournament during the pandemic. With teams and players not seeing any court action in over a year, just the chance to play again was enough reason to join the PVL. As of this writing, various PVL teams have begun their training bubbles under the auspices and approval of the GAB and the IATF. The PVL successfully organized a bubble season in late 2021 and had its non-bubble season in early 2022.

432. As of May 2022, sports have resumed, but still far from pre-pandemic levels. Pro leagues are back, but collegiate sports have been slow to return, given the higher protection needed for student-athletes. For example, the UAAP resumed but only hosted a handful of "popular" sports like men's basketball and women's volleyball. The future looks brighter, but this hope should be tempered given the current economic and political outlook of the Philippines.

814. Niel Victor C. Masoy, *New PVL Teams Give Motivation to Valdez*, The Manila Times (Apr. 6, 2021), https://www.manilatimes.net/2021/04/06/sports/top-sports/new-pvl-teams-give-motivation-to-valdez/860446.

Part VI. Safe Sport and Safe Spaces

Chapter 1. The Safe Spaces Act

433. With the terrible trend of news on physical, emotional, and sexual abuse of athletes, it is only appropriate to discuss how Philippine laws have been treating the matter. Aside from the laws discussed in the Criminal Liability Section, focus must also be given to Republic Act No. 11313 or the Safe Spaces Act of 2018 (SSA).

434. In 2018, or two years into his administration, President Duterte signed the SSA into law—which those who had known Duterte found ironic, given his history of misogynistic statements. Duterte once joked that he "should have been first" when recounting a story where convicts gang raped an Australian missionary when he was still the Mayor of Davao City[815] and once remarked that the Philippine presidency is not a job for women.[816]

435. These remarks run counter to the state policy recognized in the SSA which acknowledged the "role of women in nation-building and ensure the fundamental equality before the law of women and men"[817]—a policy likewise enshrined in the Constitution. The SSA further recognized that women must have "equality, security, safety not only in private, but also on the streets, public spaces, online, workplaces, and educational and training institutions."[818]

436. The SSA's comprehensive list of definitions set the tone for the rest of the law. Gender is defined as "a set of socially ascribed characteristics, norms, roles, attitudes, values and expectations identifying the social behavior of men and women, and the relations between them."[819] Gender identity and/or expression is

---

815. Nestor Corrales, *Duterte Rape Joke on Australian Missionary: Too Much?,* Philippine Daily Inquirer (Apr. 17, 2016), https://newsinfo.inquirer.net/779912/viral-duterte-rape-joke-on-australian-missionary.
816. Pia Ranada, *Sexist Duterte Says Philippine Presidency Not a Job for Women*, Rappler, (Jan. 14, 2021), https://www.rappler.com/nation/sexist-duterte-says-philippine-presidency-not-a-job-for-women/.
817. Safe Spaces Act, Republic Act. No. 11313, §2.
818. *Ibid.*, §3(d).
819. *Ibid.*

defined as the "personal sense of identity as characterized, among others, by manner of clothing, inclinations, and behavior in relation to masculine or feminine conventions."[820] The definition of gender identity also includes a definition of transgender as a person who "may have a male or female identity with physiological characteristics of the opposite sex."[821] Those familiar with issues regarding gender equality and transgender participation in sports will find these definitions helpful.

437. At its core, the SSA is a criminal statute. Hence, it also defines criminal acts. Stalking is a crime. It is defined as "conduct directed at a person involving the repeated visual or physical proximity, non-consensual communication, or a combination thereof that cause or will likely cause a person to fear for one's own safety or the safety of others, or to suffer emotional distress."[822] Catcalling is also now criminalized, so wolf-whistlers beware. Catcalling is "any unwanted remarks directed towards a person, commonly done in the form of wolf-whistling and misogynistic, transphobic, homophobic, and sexist slurs."[823]

438. Athletes can take refuge in the SSA in four distinct settings: public places, online spaces, in the workplace, and in education and training settings.

439. Article I of the SSA covers gender-based sexual harassment in streets and public places. Section 4 criminalizes "any unwanted and uninvited sexual actions or remarks against any person regardless of the motive for committing such action or remarks" that occur in public spaces such as streets, buildings, schools, churches, restaurants, public washrooms, and even in public utility vehicles.[824] These also include sports stadia, arenas, and other sports venues.

440. Gender-based sexual harassment in streets and public places includes:

> catcalling, wolf-whistling, unwanted invitations, misogynistic, transphobic, homophobic and sexist slurs, persistent uninvited comments or gestures on a person's appearance, relentless requests for personal details, statement of sexual comments and suggestions, public masturbation or flashing of private parts, groping, or any advances, whether verbal or physical, that is unwanted and has threatened one's sense of personal space and physical safety.[825]

441. As can be seen, the law protects against both verbal and physical abuses. Hence, spectators who heckle athletes because of their clothing or appearance may be held liable under the SSA. Shouting a homophobic slur during a game to demean an athlete—a usual occurrence in the Philippines— is also a criminal act.

---

820. *Ibid.*, §3(f).
821. *Ibid.*
822. *Ibid.*, §3(h).
823. *Ibid.*, §3(a).
824. *Ibid.*, §4 and §5.
825. *Ibid.*, §4.

442. Article II of the SSA is revolutionary in the sense that it protects against gender-based online sexual harassment. Gender-based online sexual harassment is defined as:

> acts that use information and communications technology in terrorizing and intimidating victims through physical, psychological, and emotional threats, unwanted sexual misogynistic, transphobic, homophobic and sexist remarks and comments online whether publicly or through direct and private messages, invasion of victim's privacy through cyberstalking and incessant messaging, uploading and sharing without the consent of the victim, any form of media that contains photos, voice, or video with sexual content, any unauthorized recording and sharing of any of the victim's photos, videos, or any information online, impersonating identities of victims online or posting lies about victims to harm their reputation, or filing false abuse reports to online platforms to silence victims.[826]

443. The reach of the SSA to protect against gender-based sexual harassment in online spaces is necessarily and purposefully broad. As the list of violations is not exclusive, implementation is given more flexibility, an aspect which is essential given the ephemeral nature of the internet. Online gamers, streamers, and eSports athletes will find the SSA a welcome solace, particularly given the prevalence of sexist remarks and even threats women face while gaming or streaming online. While actual conviction of online pervs still face challenges because of anonymity, the SSA is definitely a step in the right direction, at least in terms of deterrence and moral persuasion.

444. In the workplace setting, the SSA works by further strengthening the Anti-Sexual Harassment Act by criminalizing gender-based sexual harassment in the workplace. Unwelcome sexual advances (whether done verbally, physically, or via the use of technology) and sexual conduct affecting the dignity of a person are prohibited.[827] These apply to sports especially for female trainers and staff.

445. In education and training institutions, the SSA likewise strengthens the Anti-Sexual Harassment Act. Schools must adopt mechanisms to prevent gender-based sexual harassment in education and training institutions. These include assigning an officer-in-charge to accept complaints of gender-based sexual harassment[828] and implementing a grievance procedure for complaints by students and staff adopted by the school.[829] Schools must still investigate and take steps to resolve complaints, despite the desistance of the victim.[830] Hopefully, the SSA can be used by student-athletes who fall victim to unscrupulous coaches and administrators.

826. *Ibid.*, §12.
827. *Ibid.*, §16.
828. *Ibid.*, §21.
829. *Ibid.*, §21.
830. *Ibid.*

Chapter 2. Proposed POC Safe Sport Policy

446. In late 2021, the POC Athletes' Commission drafted a proposed Safe Sport Policy for the POC. Key aspects of the Safe Sport Policy were outlining the different kinds of abuses athletes may face and a proposal to create a Safe Sport Committee within the POC, along with a POC Safeguarding Officer. The Safe Sport Policy covers athletes or non-athlete participants within the jurisdiction of the POC and its member NSAs. It also includes a proposed background check for recruiting coaches, administrators, and staff. It also provides athletes with a reporting procedure and guidelines regarding the portrayal of children in the media. However, the POC has yet to approve the proposed Safe Sport Policy as of May 2022.

447. Note that the proposed Safe Sport Policy applies within the POC and its member NSAs. It does not apply to professional teams and even university teams which may draft and implement their own out of their own initiative. It will be good for these organizations to follow the lead of the Philippine Rugby Football Union, the NSA for rugby which has been instrumental in spearheading child safeguarding and safe sport within its ranks at its own initiative.

Selected Bibliography

Books

Cesario Alvero Azucena Jr., *Everyone's Labor Code* (9th ed. 2018).
Cesario Alvero Azucena Jr., *The Labor Code with Comments and Cases Vol. II* (2016).
Edgardo L. Paras, *Civil Code of the Philippines Annotated* (2008).
Ernesto Pineda, *Torts and Damages (Annotated)* (2009).
Ignatius Michael D. Ingles, *Laws for Sports and the Sporty* (2019).
Ignatius Michael D. Ingles, *Tax Made Less Taxing* (2nd ed. 2018).
Rafe Bartholomew, *Pacific Rims: Beerman Ballin' in Flip-Flops and the Philippines' Unlikely Love Affair with Basketball* (2010).

Online Articles/Sources

ABS-CBN News Staff, *"Wait is over" for PBA, PFF as order signed for practices to resume*, ABS-CBN News (July 27, 2020), https://news.abs-cbn.com/sports/07/27/20/wait-is-over-for-pba-pff-as-order-signed-for-practices-to-resume.
ABS-CBN News Staff, *LIST: The All-Time Filipino Gold Medalists in the Asian Games*, ABS-CBN News (September 2, 2018), https://news.abs-cbn.com/sports/09/02/18/list-the-all-time-filipino-gold-medalists-in-the-asian-games.
ABS-CBN News Staff, *PFF still awaiting IATF go-signal for football's return*, ABS-CBN News (June 29, 2020), https://news.abs-cbn.com/sports/06/29/20/pff-still-awaiting-iatf-go-signal-for-footballs-return.
ABS-CBN News Staff, *PSC cancels sports events, assures support for national athletes*, ABS-CBN News (April 29, 2020), https://news.abs-cbn.com/sports/04/29/20/psc-cancels-sports-events-assures-support-for-national-athletes.
ABS-CBN Sports Staff, *2019 SEA Games eSports Closes with Record Numbers*, ABS-CBN Sports (December 12, 2019), https://sports.abs-cbn.com/esports/news/2019/12/12/2019-sea-games-esports-closes-record-numbers-64330.
ACAMS Today, *Human Trafficking and Major Sporting Events: The Dark Side of the Super Bowl* (March 28, 2019), https://www.acamstoday.org/human-trafficking-and-major-sporting-events-the-dark-side-of-the-super-bowl/.
Aika Rey, *Baguio High School Basketball Coach Accused of Sexual Harassment,* Rappler (January 10, 2018), https://www.rappler.com/move-ph/193036-basketball-coach-leo-arnaiz-sexual-harassment.

Selected Bibliography

Aimee Grace Tapeceria, *PBA || Ref Edward Aquino and Calvin Abueva Incident || Alaska v. Barako || 02/17/13*, at 00:03-0:23 (February 18, 2013), https://www.youtube.com/watch?v=LhVJEVC-E9g.

Anton Roxas, *SWAG ON: The UAAP Gears Up with New Era PH*, ABS-CBN (July 29, 2018), https://sports.abs-cbn.com/uaap/news/2018/07/29/swag-on-the-uaap-gears-new-era-ph-45066.

Arnell Ozaeta, *34 Moviegoers Arrested for Not Standing up to Sing "Lupang Hinirang" Inside Cinema*, The Philippine Star (September 6, 2018), https://www.philstar.com/nation/2018/09/06/1849213/34-moviegoers-arrested-not-standing-sing-lupang-hinirang-inside-cinema.

Beatrice Go, *NCAA to Ban Foreign Players Starting Season 96 in* 2020, Rappler (June 19, 2018), https://www.rappler.com/sports/university/ncaa/205265-ban-foreign-players-imports-2020.

Beatrice Go, *FAST FACTS: Who Is Boxing World Champion Nesthy Petecio?*, Rappler (October 14, 2019), https://www.rappler.com/sports/by-sport/boxing-mma/242470-things-to-know-about-world-champion-nesthy-petecio.

Beatrice Go, *Ricky Vargas Resigns as POC President,* Rappler (June 18, 2019), https://www.rappler.com/sports/by-sport/other-sports/233331-ricky-vargas-resigns-president-philippine-olympic-committee.

Beatrice Go, *Unpaid Global FC players can seek PH football federation's assistance*, Rappler (August 5, 2020), https://www.rappler.com/sports/football/unpaid-global-fc-players-seek-assistance-philippine-football-league-federation.

Beatrice Go, *Ph Team Budget Increased for Jam-Packed 2022 Campaign*, Rappler.com (September 30, 2021), https://www.rappler.com/sports/house-senate-increase-philippine-sports-commission-2022-budget/.

Ben O. de Vera, *POGO Tax Take Drops 46 Percent to P3.91 Billion in 2021*, Philippine Daily Inquirer (April 07, 2022), https://business.inquirer.net/345482/pogo-tax-take-drops-46-percent-to-p3-91-billion-in-2021.

Camille B. Naredo, *Kiefer Ravena Suspended by FIBA over Banned Substance*, ABS-CBN News (May 28, 2018), https://news.abs-cbn.com/sports/05/28/18/kiefer-ravena-suspended-by-fiba-over-banned-substance.

Camille Elemia, *After 2 Years, Senate Finally OKs Manny Pacquiao's First Pet Bill on Boxing*, Rappler (September 10, 2018), https://www.rappler.com/sports/by-sport/boxing-mma/211638-pacquiao-bill-philippine-boxing-commision-creation-gets-senate-approval.

Carlo Pamintuan, *Amid Game-Fixing Scandal, Seven-Man CEU Triumphs in PBA D-League QFs,* TV5 ESPN (May 30, 2019), https://tv5.espn.com/basketball/story/_/id/26853624/amid-game-fixing-scandal-seven-man-ceu-triumphs.

Carlos Costa, *Games and Amusements Board Is 2017 World Boxing Council's Commission of the Year*, Games and Amusements Board, http://gab.gov.ph/wbcs-commission-of-the-year-for-2017/.

Cecilia Munoz-Palma, *Closing Remarks of the President of the Constitutional Commission at the Final Session*, Official Gazette (October 15, 1986), https://www.officialgazette.gov.ph/1986/10/15/closing-remarks-of-the-president-of-the-constitutional-commission-at-the-final-session-october-15-1986/.

Ceej Tantengco, *How Much Does It Cost to Win an Olympic Medal?*, CNN Philippines (June 17, 2019), https://www.cnnphilippines.com/life/culture/2019/6/17/cost-Olympics-Hidilyn-Diaz.html.

Christian V. Esguerra, *Why Host Countries Dominate SEA Games, Falter in Next*, ABS-CBN News (December 6, 2019), https://news.abs-cbn.com/sports/12/06/19/why-host-countries-dominate-sea-games-falter-in-next (which explains why host countries normally win the SEA Games).

CNN Staff, *PBA Allows Full Capacity Crowd Amid Alert Level 1 Shift*, CNN Philippines (March 1, 2022), https://www.cnnphilippines.com/sports/2022/3/1/PBA-full-audience-capacity-Alert-Level-1.html.

Dan Carson, *Manny Pacquiao Ring Walk: Philippines Star to Walk Out to His Own Song,* Bleach Report (May 3, 2015), https://bleacherreport.com/articles/2450147-manny-pacquiao-ring-walk-philippines-star-to-walk-out-to-his-own-song.

David Tristan Yumol, *UAAP board cancels Season 82 due to COVID-19 pandemic*, CNN Philippines (April 17, 2020), https://cnnphilippines.com/sports/2020/4/7/uaap-cancels-season-82-covid-pandemic.html.

Daxim L. Lucas, *Pagcor Imposes Moratorium on New POGO Licenses*, Philippine Daily Inquirer (August 20, 2019), https://business.inquirer.net/277179/pagcor-imposes-moratorium-on-new-pogo-licenses.

Decision, *FIBA Disciplinary Panel Established in Accordance with Article 8.1 of the FIBA Internal Regulations Governing Anti-Doping in the matter Kiefer Isaac Ravena* (May 22, 2018), https://news.abs-cbn.com/focus/05/28/18/read-fiba-timeline-of-kiefer-ravena-testing-results-suspension.

Delfin Dioquino, *GAB chief warns VisMin Super Cup, probes controversial game*, Rappler (April 14, 2021), https://www.rappler.com/sports/gab-chief-warns-vismin-super-cup-probes-controversial-game.

Delfin Dioquino, *TIMELINE: Chaos follows as UST bubble bursts*, Rappler (Sept. 10, 2020), https://www.rappler.com/sports/uaap/timeline-chaos-follows-ust-bubble.

Dennis Gasgonia, *Ricky Vargas Elected New PH Olympic Committee President*, ABS-CBN News (February 23, 2018), https://news.abs-cbn.com/sports/02/23/18/ricky-vargas-elected-new-ph-olympic-committee-president.

Department of Health Staff, *DOH & GAB Ink Agreement to Support Pinoy Boxers and Mixed Martial Artists*, Department of Health, https://portal2.doh.gov.ph/node/14969.

Department of Labor and Employment, *Frequently Asked Questions on the Revised Rules for the Issuance of Employment Permits to Foreign Nationals (D.O. No. 97-09)*, http://www.ble.dole.gov.ph/index.php/web-pages/118-alien-employment-permit (last visited May 17, 2018).

Department of Social Welfare and Development (DSWD) *Frequently Asked Questions on Clearance for Minors Abroad,* https://www.dswd.gov.ph/frequently-ask-questions-faqs/ (last visited January 22, 2020).

Games and Amusements Board, Status Update, *Clarification from the Games and Amusement Board* (January 6, 2017), https://www.facebook.com/GamesandAmusementsBoard/photos/pcb.1517528191677934/151752729834469 0/?type=3&theater (last visited May 17, 2018).

Selected Bibliography

Games and Amusements Board Staff, *Historical Background*, Games and Amusements Board, https://gab.gov.ph/historical-background/.

Games and Amusements Board Staff, *Professional Basketball and Other Professional Sports Fees and Charges*, http://gab.gov.ph/professional-basketball-and-other-professional-sports-fees-and-charges/#ProBasketball.

Games and Amusements Board & Philippine Sports Commission, *Guidelines on the Definitions of Professional Athlete and Professional Sports or Competitions*, Joint Resolution No. 2020-01, https://gab.gov.ph/wp-content/uploads/2020/10/GAB-AND-PSC-JOINT-RESOLUTION-1.pdf?fbclid=IwAR02h7yH7gFUfbM6 tQcCmM0f_N5aLVorKjWxTNc_5rMMKBTONqMaP2ibHYA (last visited May 27, 2021).

Gerry Ramos, *Does Having an NBA-Caliber Import Guarantee a PBA Title? Let's See,* Spin.ph (August 12, 2019), https://www.spin.ph/life/guide/nba-caliber-imports-who-played-in-pba-a793-20190812-lfrm2.

Gretchen Ho, *A Purpose Bigger Than Gold*, Philippine Star (January 1, 2022), https: //philstarlife.com/self/631440-hidilyn-diaz-gold.

Hegemon, *Lia Cruz: Sexual Harassment in Men's Locker Room Should Be Challenged,* Tumblr (March 9, 2012), https://hegemon.tumblr.com/post/18958840950 /lia-cruz-sexual-harassment-in-mens-locker-room.

Ignatius Michael D. Ingles, *#LetRobPlay: Explaining Rob Ricafort's Eligibility Case v. the UAAP,* Batas Sportiva (October 19, 2017), https://batassportiva.com /2017/10/19/letrobplay-explaining-rob-ricaforts-eligibility-case-vs-the-uaap/.

Ignatius Michael D. Ingles, *Equal Protection: Athletes with Disabilities and RA 10699*, Batas Sportiva (September 17, 2016), https://batassportiva.com/2016/09/ 17/equal-protection-athletes-with-disabilities-and-ra-10699/.

Ignatius Michael D. Ingles, *The FIBA Decision on the Basketbrawl: Where Do We Go From Here?*, Batas Sportiva (July 19, 2018), https://batassportiva.com/2018 /07/19/the-fiba-decision-on-the-basketbrawl-where-do-we-go-from-here/.

Ignatius Michael D. Ingles, *Hidilyn's Golden 33M: Taxable or Not?*, Batas Sportiva (July 27, 2021), https://batassportiva.com/2021/07/27/hidilyns-golden-33m-taxable-or-not/.

Ignatius Michael D. Ingles, *Keeping Sports Out of Courts: Philippine Sports Arbitration (Part III),* Batas Sportiva (October 27, 2016), https://batassportiva.com/ 2016/10/27/keeping-sports-out-of-courts-philippines-sports-arbitration-part-iii/.

Ignatius Michael D. Ingles, *Covid-19: Fortuitous Event or Not?*, Batas Sportiva (March 10 2020), https://batassportiva.com/2020/03/10/covid-19-fortuitous-event-or-not/.

Ignatius Michael D. Ingles, *Exploring 5 legal considerations of sports bubbles*, Rappler (September 15, 2020), https://www.rappler.com/sports/exploring-five-legal-considerations-of-sports-bubbles.

Ivan Stewart Saldajeno, *NCAA Season 95 ended due to Covid-19*, Philippine News Agency (March 19, 2020), https://www.pna.gov.ph/articles/1097211.

Jack Thorne, *When Do Sport Teams' Initiation Ceremonies Cross Legal Boundaries? Part 1,* Law in Sport (July 17, 2014), https://www.lawinsport.com/more/ blogs/squire-patton-boggs/item/when-do-sport-teams-initiation-ceremonies-cross -legal-boundaries-part-1.

Joaquin M. Henson, *Huelgas Pins Olympic Hopes on Kims*, The Philippine Star (January 13, 2020), https://www.philstar.com/sports/2020/01/13/1984379/huelgas-pins-olympic-hopes-kims.
Joaquin M. Henson, *Resolving NSA Disputes*, The Philippine Star (October 9, 2018), https://www.philstar.com/sports/2018/10/09/1858563/resolving-nsa-disputes.
Jodee A. Agoncillo, *Family of Minor "Raped" by Volleyball Coach Offers P100-K Reward Money*, The Philippine Daily Inquirer (January 3, 2018), https://newsinfo.inquirer.net/957184/family-of-minor-raped-by-volleyball-coach-offers-p100-k-reward-money.
Joey Villar, *Barroca Dropped from FEU for Good,* Philippine Star (September 20, 2009), https://www.philstar.com/sports/2009/09/20/506641/barroca-dropped-feu-good.
Julian Malonso, *NCAA History*, The Philippine Star, https://www.philstar.com/2011/06/01/698483/ncaa-history.
June Navarro, *PSI Preparations Go Full Blast for 2019 PH SEA Games*, Philippine Daily Inquirer (November 27, 2018), https://sports.inquirer.net/329119/psi-preparations-go-full-blast-for-2019-ph-sea-games?utm_expid=.XqNwTug2W6nwDVUSgFJXed.1.
Kathleen de Villa, *Timeline: UAAP History*, Philippine Daily Inquirer (August 31, 2019), https://business.inquirer.net/277964/timeline-uaap-history.
Lance Agcaoili, *PVL team owners agree pro status will take league to new heights*, Spin.ph (November 14, 2020), https://www.spin.ph/volleyball/pvl/pvl-team-owners-agree-pro-status-will-take-league-to-new-heights-a2522-20201114.
Lance Agcaoili, *EJ Obiena, Patafa, Reach Settlement After Successful Mediation-PSC*, Philippine Inquirer (March 30, 2022), https://sports.inquirer.net/456608/ej-obiena-patafa-reach-settlement-after-successful-mediation-psc.
Ma. Angelica Garcia, *PBA suspends games indefinitely due to COVID-19 threat*, GMA News Online (March 11, 2020), https://www.gmanetwork.com/news/sports/basketball/729223/pba-suspends-games-indefinitely-due-to-covid-19/story/.
Mara Cepeda, *Pacquiao Top Absentee in Congress*, Rappler (July 27, 2016), https://www.rappler.com/nation/140143-pacquiao-attendance-last-session-16th-congress.
Margarita C. Gonzalez & Thea Unson, LM, *OSA to Improve Safety Measures after Undergraduate Student's Passing*, The Guidon (October 20, 2018), http://www.theguidon.com/1112/main/2018/10/lm-osa-improve-safety-measures-undergraduate-students-passing/.
Marc Anthony Reyes, *SEA Games: Carlos Yulo Gets Fifth Gold to Lead Ph Gymnastics to Best Finish in Recent Years*, Philippine Daily Inquirer (May 16, 2022), https://sports.inquirer.net/462741/sea-games-carlos-yulo-gets-fifth-gold-to-lead-ph-gymnastics-to-best-finish-in-recent-years.
Mark Giongco, *Nesthy Petecio Takes Home Olympic Silver in Boxing*, Philippine Inquirer (August 3, 2021), https://sports.inquirer.net/432030/nesthy-petecio-takes-home-olympic-silver-in-boxing.
Mark Edward Lopez, *Defining the 2010s: Emergence of PVL, PSL and Spikers' Turf, Fox Sports PH* (January 1, 2020), https://www.foxsports.ph/volleyball/1057564/defining-the-2010s-emergence-of-pvl-psl-and-spikers-turf/.

Michael Angelo S. Murillo, *Standout Moments (2)*, Business World (January 1, 2019), https://www.bworldonline.com/standout-moments-2/.

Michelle Abad, *Timeline: Duterte Against ABS-CBN's Franchise Renewal*, Rappler (January 17, 2020), https://www.rappler.com/newsbreak/iq/249550-timeline-duterte-against-abs-cbn-franchise-renewal.

Moch. Fiqih Prawira Adjie, *2020 ASEAN Para Games official canceled*, The Jakarta Post (May 9, 2020), https://www.thejakartapost.com/news/2020/05/09/2020-asean-para-games-officially-canceled.html.

Nestor Corrales, *Duterte Rape Joke on Australian Missionary: Too Much?*, Philippine Daily Inquirer (April 17, 2016), https://newsinfo.inquirer.net/779912/viral-duterte-rape-joke-on-australian-missionary.

Nestlé MILO® Staff, *Greatest Milo Moments*, Nestlé, https://www.milo.com.ph/history.

Nick Atkin, *Fiba Decision on Philippines v. Australia Brawl: 13 Basketball Players Suspended after Fight at World Cup 2019 Qualifier*, South China Morning Post (July 19, 2018), https://www.scmp.com/sport/other-sport/article/2155986/philippines-v-australia-basketball-brawl-fiba-suspends-13-players.

Niel Victor C. Masoy, *Abanse Negrense A rules 2021 PSL Beach Volley*, The Manila Times (March 1, 2021), https://www.manilatimes.net/2021/03/01/sports/sports-top/abanse-negrense-a-rules-2021-psl-beach-volley/846192/.

Niel Victor C. Masoy, *New PVL teams give motivation to Valdez*, The Manila Times (April 6, 2021), https://www.manilatimes.net/2021/04/06/sports/top-sports/new-pvl-teams-give-motivation-to-valdez/860446.

Nissi Icasiano, *UFC Rep Denies Drug Testing Led to Manila Event's Cancellatio*n, Rappler (October 8. 2016), https://www.rappler.com/sports/by-sport/other-sports/148498-ufc-drug-testing-manila.

Norman Lee Riego, *Best of Five Series: The Rivalry That Gave Birth to the PBA, ABS-CBN Sports* (April 12, 2015), http://sports.abs-cbn.com/basketball/news/2015/04/12/best-of-five-series-the-rivalry-gave-birth-pba-1744.

Office of the Chairman, *Accomplishment Report January–June 2017*, Games and Amusements Board, http://gab.gov.ph/wp-content/uploads/2017/06/2017_AnnAccomRep.pdf.

Ohmer Bautista, *PVL to start 2020 Season with Open Conference, mulls opening day reset*, Tiebreaker Times (April 19, 2020), https://tiebreakertimes.com.ph/tbt/pvl-start-2020-season-open-conference-mulls-opening-day-reset/183611.

Paul McLeod, *Filipino Champions Said to Be Overage: Little League: Newspaper in Philippines Says Officials Faked Documents and Lied about Birth Dates at World Series.*, Los Angeles Times (September 4, 1992), https://www.latimes.com/archives/la-xpm-1992-09-04-sp-6363-story.html.

Philip Matel, *Meralco Bolts all set to leave for Ilocos Norte training camp on Saturday*, ESPN (May 13, 2021), https://tv5.espn.com/basketball/pba/story/_/id/31436351/bolts-set-hold-training-camp-ilocos-norte.

Philippine Amusement and Gaming Corporation Staff, *Offshore Gaming Regulatory Manual*, Philippine Amusement and Gaming Corporation (July 3, 2018) 4, http://www.pagcor.ph/regulatory/pdf/offshore/Offshore-Gaming-Regulatory-Manual.pdf.

Philippine Amusement and Gaming Corporation Staff, *Our Corporate Profile*, Philippine Amusement and Gaming Corporation, http://www.pagcor.ph/pagcor-corporate-profile.php.

Philippine Olympic Committee Staff, *About the POC*, Philippine Olympic Committee, https://www.olympic.ph/about-the-poc.

Philippine Olympic Committee Staff, *Our NSAs*, Philippine Olympic Committee, https://www.olympic.ph/national-sports-association-regular-members/.

Philippine Olympic Committee, *POC Code of Ethics*, Tech Cellar, http://www.techcellar.com/olympic/wp-content/uploads/2015/10/codeofethics.pdf?__cf_chl_jschl_tk__=220e64ca9a73409b2cad93af73e194f75a2576e7-1579500784-0-AY6y4OLyZFiIKYZw0qxzxkjIFfrUeBqV3OGaX0si7Gl2kVNQkPGA74T0feQih8B1y7eAvbeurof7cBCBHFL-UxRabwn5bTWedW106M8lGA2vcD8OvjoEt3VGS8uCrB_XzM6eYahDMzuiYvk7-9hiJzUnTvT8e_0Iqo9tyKsaSHzyOGPuSQXe3mIMGViZA7JdNYcYqjWk2bCW9KDkqbf1hWAyDUpKFXmnZ2Sr0cHGVaZ4tRusDY40CqifaYFmXxLcOehlG4jDsYpeBoiXLnrTCA_9mW8XD_D-j4TZ4iHniuL96aN3RdqKh8GeXyXK6bUoq_M93-QK3RZ1gxPqJ5cXbTM.

Philippine Olympic Committee Ethics Commission, *Rules of Procedure Governing the Investigation of Cases Brought Before the POC Ethics Commission*, Philippine Olympic Committee, https://web.archive.org/web/20130129212257/http://www.olympic.ph/procedure.pdf.

Philippine Olympic Committee Ethics Commission, *Statutes of the POC Ethics Commission*, Philippine Olympic Committee, https://web.archive.org/web/20130108210349/http://www.olympic.ph/statutes.pdf.

Philippine Sports Commission, *Policy Directives of the Philippine Sports Commission on COVID-19* (March 12, 2020), https://www.facebook.com/PhlSportsCommission/posts/policy-directives-ofphilippine-sports-commission-on-covid-19pursuant-to-presiden/2983875238302430/ (last visited May 26, 2021).

Pia Ranada, *Sexist Duterte Says Philippine Presidency Not A Job for Women*, Rappler, (January 14, 2021), https://www.rappler.com/nation/sexist-duterte-says-philippine-presidency-not-a-job-for-women/

Rafe Bartholomew, *A Nation's Passion Lives in a Rivalry of Green v. Blue*, The New York Times (September 23, 2007), http://www.nytimes.com/2007/09/23/sports/23rivalry.html.

Randolph B. Leongson, *"Poaching" Attempts Cited as Reason Behind UST Benching of Rhenz Abando,* Spin.ph (October 17, 2019), https://www.spin.ph/basketball/uaap-men/poaching-attempts-cited-as-reason-behind-ust-benching-of-rhenz-abando-a2437-20191017.

Rappler, *FAQs: Rappler's SEC Case,* https://www.rappler.com/about-rappler/about-us/194165-frequently-asked-questions-rappler-sec-case (January 28, 2018).

Rappler, *POC to End NSA Disputes with New Resolution Framework* (January 15, 2019), https://www.rappler.com/sports/by-sport/other-sports/220989-philippine-olympic-committee-end-nsa-disputes-new-resolution-framework.

Reuben Terrado, *MPBL Suspends Soccsksargen Marlins for Alleged Game-Fixing,* Spin.ph Sports (November 4, 2019), https://www.spin.ph/basketball/mpbl-soccsksargen-marlins-suspended-alleged-game-fixing-a795-20191104.

Selected Bibliography

Reuben Terrado, *PSC Approves P600 Million Budget for NSAs with P220M Going to "Top-Tier Sports,"* Spin.ph (March 29, 2018), https://www.spin.ph/multisport/psc-600-million-budget-nsas-2018-top-tier-sports.

Ronnie Nathanielsz, *Olympic Stories: Onyok Velasco, Yahoo! News* (July 10, 2012), https://sg.news.yahoo.com/olympic-stories--onyok-velasco.html.

Sherrie Ann Torres, *4 Senators Record Perfect Session Attendance*, ABS-CBN News (June 5, 2018), https://news.abs-cbn.com/news/06/05/18/4-senators-record-perfect-session-attendance.

Spin.ph, *How Much Can PBA Players Make in Terms of Bonuses? See Spin.ph Q&A,* https://www.spin.ph/basketball/pba/how-much-do-pba-players-make-in-terms-of-bonuses-read-spin-q- (October 26, 2015).

Spin.ph, *PESO Named Official National Sports Association for eSports in the Philippines*, Spin.ph (October 16, 2020), https://www.spin.ph/esports/peso-named-official-nsa-for-esports-in-the-philippines-a1373-20201016.

Spot.ph Staff, *Updated: Executive, 52, Dies in Ironman 70.3 Triathlon in Cam Sur*, Spot.ph (August 23, 2009), https://www.spot.ph/newsfeatures/29497/executive-drownin-cwc-ironman-in-cam-sur.

SunStar Philippines Staff, *Triathlete Dies in Ironman's Swim Leg*, SunStar Philippines (August 7, 2017), https://www.sunstar.com.ph/article/157164.

The Wires, *Mikee Romero Wants Bill Banning Foreign Players in College Leagues*, Spin.ph (September 30, 2019), https://www.spin.ph/basketball/uaap-men/mikee-romero-files-bill-seeking-ban-on-foreign-players-in-college-leagues-a1373-2019 0930.

Victor Barreiro Jr., *Valve Rescinds PH "Dota 2" Tournament's Major Designation*, Rappler (January 5, 2018), https://www.rappler.com/technology/news/192948-valve-revokes-ph-dota-2-tournament-major-designation.

Vignesh Raghuram, *Top 10 Highest-Earning Filipino eSports Players of All Time*, AFK Gaming (September 3, 2019), https://afkgaming.com/articles/esports/Blogs/2371-Top-10-highest-earning-Filipino-esports-players-of-all-time.

Welcome to PFL!, *Philippines Football League*, https://www.pfltv.ph/info.

Law Journals

Anna Carmi Calsado-Amoroso & Patrick Edward L. Balisong, *In or Out: Gaps in Philippine Immigration Law in Relation to Foreign Athletes and Sports Leagues Regulations—Migration and Human Rights Issues,* 63 Ateneo L. J. 689, 799 (2019).

Ignatius Michael D. Ingles, *Are You Sure You Want to Post That? Examining Student Social Media Use and Constitutional Rights*, 59 Ateneo L. J. 723 (2014).

Ignatius Michael D. Ingles, *Philippine Sports Torts: Adopting a Standard of Care for Sports Competitions and Establishing Vicarious Liability for Professional Coaches*, 27 Marq. Sports L. Rev. 1 (2016).

Ignatius Michael D. Ingles & Katrina Bianca Louise S. Diploma, *Strength in Unity: Reviving the PBA Union,* 43 Ateneo L. J. 689 (2019).

Ignatius Michael D. Ingles, *Playing for Wages: Defining the Legal Relationship Between Professional Athlete and Team, a Sports Law Perspective on Philippine Labor Law,* 59 Ateneo L.J. 798 (2014).

Lolibeth R. Medrano & John Paulo Vicencio, *Under the Shadows of Trademark: The Current State of Publicity Rights in the Philippines,* 63 Ateneo L. J. 689 (2019).

Selected Bibliography

Table of Cases

Table of Statutes

Index

The numbers here refer to paragraph numbers.

Index